卞尺丹几乙し丹卞と
Translated Language Learning

The Communist Manifesto

البيان الشيوعي

Karl Marx & Friedrich Engels

كارل ماركس وفريدريك انجلز

English / العربية

Published by Tranzlaty
ISBN: 978-1-83566-461-2
Original text by Karl Marx and Friedrich Engels
The Communist Manifesto
First published in 1848
www.tranzlaty.com

Introduction
مقدمة

A spectre is haunting Europe — the spectre of Communism

شبح يطارد أوروبا - شبح الشيوعية

All the Powers of old Europe have entered into a holy alliance to exorcise this spectre

دخلت جميع قوى أوروبا القديمة في تحالف مقدس لطرد هذا الشبح.

Pope and Czar, Metternich and Guizot, French Radicals and German police-spies

البابا والقيصر ، مترنيخ وجيزو ، الراديكاليون الفرنسيون وجواسيس الشرطة الألمانية

Where is the party in opposition that has not been decried as Communistic by its opponents in power?

أين هو الحزب المعارض الذي لم يتم شجبه على أنه شيوعي من قبل خصومه في السلطة؟

Where is the Opposition that has not hurled back the branding reproach of Communism, against the more advanced opposition parties?

أين هي المعارضة التي لم تتخلص من اللوم الشيوعي ضد أحزاب المعارضة الأكثر تقدما؟

And where is the party that has not made the accusation against its reactionary adversaries?

وأين هو الحزب الذي لم يوجه الاتهام إلى خصومه الرجعيين؟

Two things result from this fact

هناك أمران ينتج عن هذه الحقيقة

I. Communism is already acknowledged by all European Powers to be itself a Power

I. الشيوعية معترف بها بالفعل من قبل جميع القوى الأوروبية لتكون هي نفسها قوة

II. It is high time that Communists should openly, in the face of the whole world, publish their views, aims and tendencies

لقد حان الوقت لأن ينشر الشيوعيون علانية ، في مواجهة العالم بأسره ، وجهات نظرهم وأهدافهم وميولهم.

they must meet this nursery tale of the Spectre of
Communism with a Manifesto of the party itself

يجب أن يقابلوا هذه الحكاية الحاضنة لشبح الشيوعية ببيان للحزب نفسه

To this end, Communists of various nationalities have
assembled in London and sketched the following Manifesto

تحقيقا لهذه الغاية ، اجتمع الشيوعيون من مختلف الجنسيات في لندن
ورسموا البيان التالي

this manifesto is to be published in the English, French,
German, Italian, Flemish and Danish languages

ينشر هذا البيان باللغات الإنجليزية والفرنسية والألمانية والإيطالية
والفلمنكية والدنماركية

And now it is to be published in all the languages that
Tranzlaty offers

والآن سيتم نشره بجميع اللغات التي تقدمها Tranzlaty

Bourgeois and the Proletarians
البرجوازية والبروليتاريون

The history of all hitherto existing societies is the history of class struggles

تاريخ جميع المجتمعات القائمة حتى الآن هو تاريخ الصراعات الطبقية

Freeman and slave, patrician and plebeian, lord and serf, guild-master and journeyman

حر وعبد ، أرستقراطي وعام ، سيد وقنان ، سيد نقابة ورجل رحلة

in a word, oppressor and oppressed

في كلمة واحدة ، ظالم ومظلوم

these social classes stood in constant opposition to one another

وقفت هذه الطبقات الاجتماعية في معارضة دائمة لبعضها البعض

they carried on an uninterrupted fight. Now hidden, now open

واصلوا قتالا متواصلا. مخفي الآن ، مفتوح الآن

a fight that either ended in a revolutionary re-constitution of society at large

معركة انتهت إما بإعادة تشكيل ثوري للمجتمع ككل

or a fight that ended in the common ruin of the contending classes

أو معركة انتهت بالخراب المشترك للطبقات المتنافسة

let us look back to the earlier epochs of history

دعونا ننظر إلى الوراء إلى العصور السابقة من التاريخ

we find almost everywhere a complicated arrangement of society into various orders

نجد في كل مكان تقريبا ترتيبا معقدا للمجتمع في أوامر مختلفة

there has always been a manifold gradation of social rank

كان هناك دائما تدرج متعدد للرتبة الاجتماعية

In ancient Rome we have patricians, knights, plebeians, slaves

في روما القديمة لدينا الأرستقراطيين والفرسان والعامة والعبيد

in the Middle Ages: feudal lords, vassals, guild-masters, journeymen, apprentices, serfs

في العصور الوسطى: اللوردات الإقطاعيون ، التابعون ، سادة النقابات ، الرحالة ، المتدربون ، الأقنان

in almost all of these classes, again, subordinate gradations

في جميع هذه الفئات تقريبا ، مرة أخرى ، التدرجات الثانوية

The modern Bourgeoisie society has sprouted from the ruins of feudal society

لقد نبت المجتمع البرجوازي الحديث من أنقاض المجتمع الإقطاعي

but this new social order has not done away with class antagonisms

لكن هذا النظام الاجتماعي الجديد لم يتخلص من العداوات الطبقية.

It has but established new classes and new conditions of oppression

لكنها أنشأت طبقات جديدة وظروفا جديدة من الاضطهاد.

it has established new forms of struggle in place of the old ones

لقد أنشأت أشكالا جديدة من النضال بدلا من الأشكال القديمة

however, the epoch we find ourselves in possesses one distinctive feature

ومع ذلك ، فإن الحقبة التي نجد أنفسنا فيها تمتلك سمة مميزة واحدة

the epoch of the Bourgeoisie has simplified the class antagonisms

لقد بسط عصر البرجوازية التناقضات الطبقية

Society as a whole is more and more splitting up into two great hostile camps

المجتمع ككل ينقسم أكثر فأكثر إلى معسكرين معاديين كبيرين

two great social classes directly facing each other: Bourgeoisie and Proletariat

طبقتان اجتماعيتان كبيرتان تواجهان بعضهما البعض مباشرة: البرجوازية والبروليتاريا

From the serfs of the Middle Ages sprang the chartered burghers of the earliest towns

من أقنان العصور الوسطى نشأ البرغر المستأجرون في المدن الأولى

From these burgesses the first elements of the Bourgeoisie were developed

من هذه البرجيس تم تطوير العناصر الأولى للبرجوازية

The discovery of America and the rounding of the Cape

اكتشاف أمريكا وتقريب كيب

these events opened up fresh ground for the rising
Bourgeoisie

فتحت هذه الأحداث آفاقا جديدة للبرجوازية الصاعدة

The East-Indian and Chinese markets, the colonisation of
America, trade with the colonies

الأسواق الهندية الشرقية والصينية ، استعمار أمريكا ، التجارة مع
المستعمرات

the increase in the means of exchange and in commodities
generally

الزيادة في وسائل التبادل وفي السلع بشكل عام

these events gave to commerce, navigation, and industry an
impulse never before known

أعطت هذه الأحداث للتجارة والملاحة والصناعة دفعة لم تكن معروفة من
قبل

it gave rapid development to the revolutionary element in
the tottering feudal society

أعطت تطورا سريعا للعنصر الثوري في المجتمع الإقطاعي المترنح

closed guilds had monopolised the feudal system of
industrial production

احتكرت النقابات المغلقة النظام الإقطاعي للإنتاج الصناعي

but this no longer sufficed for the growing wants of the new
markets

لكن هذا لم يعد كافيا للاحتياجات المتزايدة للأسواق الجديدة

The manufacturing system took the place of the feudal
system of industry

حل نظام التصنيع محل النظام الإقطاعي للصناعة

The guild-masters were pushed on one side by the
manufacturing middle class

تم دفع سادة النقابة على جانب واحد من قبل الطبقة الوسطى الصناعية

division of labour between the different corporate guilds
vanished

اختفى تقسيم العمل بين نقابات الشركات المختلفة

the division of labour penetrated each single workshop

اخترق تقسيم العمل كل ورشة عمل واحدة

Meantime, the markets kept ever growing, and the demand ever rising

في غضون ذلك ، استمرت الأسواق في النمو ، والطلب في ارتفاع مستمر

Even factories no longer sufficed to meet the demands

حتى المصانع لم تعد كافية لتلبية الطلبات

Thereupon, steam and machinery revolutionised industrial production

بعد ذلك ، أحدث البخار والآلات ثورة في الإنتاج الصناعي

The place of manufacture was taken by the giant, Modern Industry

تم أخذ مكان التصنيع من قبل الصناعة الحديثة العملاقة

the place of the industrial middle class was taken by industrial millionaires

تم أخذ مكان الطبقة الوسطى الصناعية من قبل أصحاب الملايين الصناعيين

the place of leaders of whole industrial armies were taken by the modern Bourgeoisie

تم أخذ مكان قادة الجيوش الصناعية بأكملها من قبل البرجوازية الحديثة

the discovery of America paved the way for modern industry to establish the world market

اكتشاف أمريكا مهد الطريق للصناعة الحديثة لتأسيس السوق العالمية

This market gave an immense development to commerce, navigation, and communication by land

أعطى هذا السوق تطورا هائلا للتجارة والملاحة والاتصالات عن طريق البر

This development has, in its time, reacted on the extension of industry

وقد تفاعل هذا التطور ، في وقته ، مع امتداد الصناعة

it reacted in proportion to how industry extended, and how commerce, navigation and railways extended

كان رد فعلها متناسبا مع كيفية توسع الصناعة ، وكيف امتدت التجارة والملاحة والسكك الحديدية

in the same proportion that the Bourgeoisie developed, they increased their capital

بنفس النسبة التي طورتها البرجوازية ، زادوا رؤوس أموالهم

and the Bourgeoisie pushed into the background every class
handed down from the Middle Ages

ودفعت البرجوازية إلى الخلفية كل طبقة متوارثة من العصور الوسطى

therefore the modern Bourgeoisie is itself the product of a
long course of development

لذلك فإن البرجوازية الحديثة هي نفسها نتاج مسار طويل من التطور

we see it is a series of revolutions in the modes of
production and of exchange

نرى أنها سلسلة من الثورات في أنماط الإنتاج والتبادل

Each developmental Bourgeoisie step was accompanied by a
corresponding political advance

رافق كل خطوة برجوازية تنموية تقدم سياسي مقابل

An oppressed class under the sway of the feudal nobility

طبقة مضطهدة تحت سيطرة النبلاء الإقطاعيين

an armed and self-governing association in the mediaeval
commune

جمعية مسلحة وذاتية الحكم في بلدية العصور الوسطى

here, an independent urban republic (as in Italy and
Germany)

هنا ، جمهورية حضرية مستقلة (كما هو الحال في إيطاليا وألمانيا)

there, a taxable "third estate" of the monarchy (as in France)

هناك ، "عقار ثالث" خاضع للضريبة من النظام الملكي (كما هو الحال في
فرنسا)

afterwards, in the period of manufacture proper

بعد ذلك ، في فترة الصنع المناسبة

the Bourgeoisie served either the semi-feudal or the absolute
monarchy

خدمت البرجوازية إما الملكية شبه الإقطاعية أو الملكية المطلقة

or the Bourgeoisie acted as a counterpoise against the
nobility

أو عملت البرجوازية كموازنة مضادة ضد النبلاء

and, in fact, the Bourgeoisie was a corner-stone of the great
monarchies in general

وفي الواقع ، كانت البرجوازية حجر الزاوية في الملكيات الكبرى بشكل
عام

but Modern Industry and the world-market established itself since then

لكن الصناعة الحديثة والسوق العالمية رسخت نفسها منذ ذلك الحين

and the Bourgeoisie has conquered for itself exclusive political sway

وقد غزت البرجوازية لنفسها نفوذا سياسيا حصريا

it achieved this political sway through the modern representative State

حققت هذا النفوذ السياسي من خلال الدولة التمثيلية الحديثة

The executives of the modern State are but a management committee

إن المديرين التنفيذيين للدولة الحديثة ليسوا سوى لجنة إدارية

and they manage the common affairs of the whole of the Bourgeoisie

ويديرون الشؤون المشتركة للبرجوازية بأسرها.

The Bourgeoisie, historically, has played a most revolutionary part

لعبت البرجوازية ، تاريخيا ، دورا ثوريا

wherever it got the upper hand, it put an end to all feudal, patriarchal, and idyllic relations

أينما كانت له اليد العليا ، فقد وضع حدا لجميع العلاقات الإقطاعية والأبوية والشاعرية.

It has pitilessly torn asunder the motley feudal ties that bound man to his "natural superiors"

لقد مزقت بلا شفقة الروابط الإقطاعية المتنافرة التي ربطت الإنسان ب "رؤسائه الطبيعيين"

and it has left remaining no nexus between man and man, other than naked self-interest

ولم تترك أي صلة بين الإنسان والإنسان ، بخلاف المصلحة الذاتية المجردة

man's relations with one another have become nothing more than callous "cash payment"

أصبحت علاقات الإنسان مع بعضها البعض ليست أكثر من "دفع نقدي" قاس

It has drowned the most heavenly ecstasies of religious fervour

لقد أغرقت أكثر النشوة السماوية من الحماسة الدينية

it has drowned chivalrous enthusiasm and philistine sentimentalism

لقد أغرقت الحماس الشهم والعاطفة الفلسطينية

it has drowned these things in the icy water of egotistical calculation

لقد أغرقت هذه الأشياء في المياه الجليدية للحساب الأناني

It has resolved personal worth into exchangeable value

لقد حلت القيمة الشخصية إلى قيمة قابلة للاستبدال

it has replaced the numberless and indefeasible chartered freedoms

لقد حلت محل الحريات المستأجرة التي لا تعد ولا تحصى ولا يمكن التخلص منها

and it has set up a single, unconscionable freedom; Free Trade

وأقامت حرية واحدة غير معقولة. التجارة الحرة

In one word, it has done this for exploitation

في كلمة واحدة ، لقد فعلت ذلك للاستغلال

exploitation veiled by religious and political illusions

استغلال محجوب بالأوهام الدينية والسياسية

exploitation veiled by naked, shameless, direct, brutal exploitation

استغلال محجوب باستغلال عار ووقح ومباشر ووحشي

the Bourgeoisie has stripped the halo off every previously honoured and revered occupation

لقد جردت البرجوازية الهالة من كل احتلال تم تكريمه وتبجيله سابقا

the physician, the lawyer, the priest, the poet, and the man of science

الطبيب والمحامي والكاهن والشاعر ورجل العلم

it has converted these distinguished workers into its paid wage labourers

لقد حولت هؤلاء العمال المتميزين إلى عمالها بأجر

The Bourgeoisie has torn the sentimental veil away from the family

لقد مزقت البرجوازية الحجاب العاطفي بعيدا عن الأسرة

and it has reduced the family relation to a mere money relation

وقد اختزلت العلاقة الأسرية إلى مجرد علاقة مالية

the brutal display of vigour in the Middle Ages which Reactionists so much admire

العرض الوحشي للقوة في العصور الوسطى التي يعجب بها الرجعيون كثيرا

even this found its fitting complement in the most slothful indolence

حتى هذا وجد مكمله المناسب في الكسل الأكثر كسلا

The Bourgeoisie has disclosed how all this came to pass

لقد كشفت البرجوازية كيف حدث كل هذا

The Bourgeoisie have been the first to show what man's activity can bring about

كانت البرجوازية أول ما أظهر ما يمكن أن يحققه نشاط الإنسان

It has accomplished wonders far surpassing Egyptian pyramids, Roman aqueducts, and Gothic cathedrals

لقد أنجزت عجائب تفوق بكثير الأهرامات المصرية والقنوات الرومانية والكاتدرائيات القوطية

and it has conducted expeditions that put in the shade all former Exoduses of nations and crusades

وقد أجرت حملات وضعت في الظل جميع هجرات الأمم والحروب الصليبية السابقة

The Bourgeoisie cannot exist without constantly revolutionising the instruments of production

لا يمكن للبرجوازية أن توجد دون إحداث ثورة مستمرة في أدوات الإنتاج

and thereby it cannot exist without its relations to production

وبالتالي لا يمكن أن توجد بدون علاقاتها بالإنتاج

and therefore it cannot exist without its relations to society

وبالتالي لا يمكن أن توجد بدون علاقاتها بالمجتمع

all earlier industrial classes had one condition in common

كان لدى جميع الفئات الصناعية السابقة شرط واحد مشترك

they relied on the conservation of the old modes of production

اعتمدوا على الحفاظ على أنماط الإنتاج القديمة

but the Bourgeoisie brought with it a completely new dynamic

لكن البرجوازية جلبت معها ديناميكية جديدة تماما.

Constant revolutionizing of production and uninterrupted disturbance of all social conditions

ثورة مستمرة في الإنتاج واضطراب مستمر لجميع الظروف الاجتماعية

this everlasting uncertainty and agitation distinguishes the Bourgeoisie epoch from all earlier ones

هذا الغموض والهياج الأبدي يميز عصر البرجوازية عن جميع الحقبة السابقة.

previous relations with production came with ancient and venerable prejudices and opinions

جاءت العلاقات السابقة مع الإنتاج مع التحيزات والآراء القديمة والموقرة

but all of these fixed, fast-frozen relations are swept away

لكن كل هذه العلاقات الثابتة والمجمدة بسرعة قد جرفت

all new-formed relations become antiquated before they can ossify

تصبح جميع العلاقات الجديدة قديمة قبل أن تتحجر

All that is solid melts into air, and all that is holy is profaned

كل ما هو صلب يذوب في الهواء ، وكل ما هو مقدس يدنس

man is at last compelled to face with sober senses, his real conditions of life

يضطر الإنسان أخيرا إلى مواجهة حواسه الرصينة ، ظروف حياته الحقيقية

and he is compelled to face his relations with his kind

وهو مضطر لمواجهة علاقاته مع نوعه

The Bourgeoisie constantly needs to expand its markets for its products

تحتاج البرجوازية باستمرار إلى توسيع أسواقها لمنتجاتها

and, because of this, the Bourgeoisie is chased over the whole surface of the globe

وبسبب هذا ، يتم مطاردة البرجوازية على كامل سطح الكرة الأرضية

The Bourgeoisie must nestle everywhere, settle everywhere, establish connections everywhere

يجب على البرجوازية أن تعشش في كل مكان ، وتستقر في كل مكان ، وتقيم روابط في كل مكان

The Bourgeoisie must create markets in every corner of the world to exploit

يجب على البرجوازية إنشاء أسواق في كل ركن من أركان العالم لاستغلالها

the production and consumption in every country has been given a cosmopolitan character

لقد تم إعطاء الإنتاج والاستهلاك في كل بلد طابعا عالميا

the chagrin of Reactionists is palpable, but it has carried on regardless

استياء الرجعيين واضح ، لكنه استمر بغض النظر عن

The Bourgeoisie have drawn from under the feet of industry the national ground on which it stood

لقد استمدت البرجوازية من تحت أقدام الصناعة الأرضية الوطنية التي وقفت عليها

all old-established national industries have been destroyed, or are daily being destroyed

تم تدمير جميع الصناعات الوطنية القديمة ، أو يتم تدميرها يوميا

all old-established national industries are dislodged by new industries

يتم إزاحة جميع الصناعات الوطنية القديمة من قبل الصناعات الجديدة

their introduction becomes a life and death question for all civilised nations

يصبح إدخالها مسألة حياة أو موت لجميع الأمم المتحضرة

they are dislodged by industries that no longer work up indigenous raw material

يتم إزاحتهم من قبل الصناعات التي لم تعد تعمل في المواد الخام الأصلية

instead, these industries pull raw materials from the remotest zones

بدلا من ذلك ، تقوم هذه الصناعات بسحب المواد الخام من المناطق النائية

industries whose products are consumed, not only at home, but in every quarter of the globe

الصناعات التي يتم استهلاك منتجاتها ، ليس فقط في المنزل ، ولكن في كل ربع من العالم

In place of the old wants, satisfied by the productions of the country, we find new wants

بدلا من الرغبات القديمة ، التي ترضيها إنتاجات البلد ، نجد رغبات جديدة

these new wants require for their satisfaction the products of distant lands and climes

هذه الرغبات الجديدة تتطلب لإشباعها منتجات الأراضي والمناخات البعيدة

In place of the old local and national seclusion and self-sufficiency, we have trade

بدلا من العزلة المحلية والوطنية القديمة والاكتفاء الذاتي ، لدينا تجارة

international exchange in every direction; universal inter-dependence of nations

التبادل الدولي في كل اتجاه ؛ الترابط العالمي بين الأمم

and just as we have dependency on materials, so we are dependent on intellectual production

وكما أننا نعتمد على المواد، كذلك نحن نعتمد على الإنتاج الفكري.

The intellectual creations of individual nations become common property

تصبح الإبداعات الفكرية للدول الفردية ملكية مشتركة

National one-sidedness and narrow-mindedness become more and more impossible

الانحياز الوطني وضيق الأفق يصبحان مستحيلين أكثر فأكثر

and from the numerous national and local literatures, there arises a world literature

ومن العديد من الآداب الوطنية والمحلية ، ينشأ أدب عالمي

by the rapid improvement of all instruments of production

من خلال التحسين السريع لجميع أدوات الإنتاج

by the immensely facilitated means of communication

من خلال وسائل الاتصال الميسرة بشكل كبير

The Bourgeoisie draws all (even the most barbarian nations) into civilisation

البرجوازية تجذب الجميع (حتى أكثر الأمم بربرية) إلى الحضارة

The cheap prices of its commodities; the heavy artillery that batters down all Chinese walls

الأسعار الرخيصة لسلعها. المدفعية الثقيلة التي تضرب جميع الجدران الصينية

the barbarians' intensely obstinate hatred of foreigners is forced to capitulate

كراهية البرابرة العنيدة بشدة للأجانب مجبرة على الاستسلام

It compels all nations, on pain of extinction, to adopt the Bourgeoisie mode of production

إنه يجبر جميع الأمم ، تحت طائلة الانقراض ، على تبني نمط الإنتاج البرجوازي

it compels them to introduce what it calls civilisation into their midst

إنه يجبرهم على إدخال ما يسميه الحضارة في وسطهم

The Bourgeoisie force the barbarians to become Bourgeoisie themselves

البرجوازية تجبر البرابرة على أن يصبحوا برجوازيين بأنفسهم

in a word, the Bourgeoisie creates a world after its own image

باختصار ، تخلق البرجوازية عالما على صورتها الخاصة

The Bourgeoisie has subjected the countryside to the rule of the towns

أخضعت البرجوازية الريف لحكم المدن

It has created enormous cities and greatly increased the urban population

لقد خلقت مدنا هائلة وزادت بشكل كبير من عدد سكان الحضر

it rescued a considerable part of the population from the idiocy of rural life

أنقذت جزءا كبيرا من السكان من حماقة الحياة الريفية

but it has made those in the the countryside dependent on the towns

لكنها جعلت أولئك الذين يعيشون في الريف يعتمدون على المدن.

and likewise, it has made the barbarian countries dependent on the civilised ones

وبالمثل ، فقد جعلت الدول البربرية تعتمد على الدول المتحضرة

nations of peasants on nations of Bourgeoisie, the East on the West

أمم الفلاحين على أمم البرجوازية والشرق على الغرب

The Bourgeoisie does away with the scattered state of the population more and more

البرجوازية تتخلص أكثر فأكثر من حالة السكان المتناثرة

It has agglomerated production, and has concentrated property in a few hands

لديها إنتاج متكتل ، وركزت الممتلكات في أيدي قليلة

The necessary consequence of this was political centralisation

وكانت النتيجة الضرورية لذلك هي المركزية السياسية.

there had been independent nations and loosely connected provinces

كانت هناك دول مستقلة ومقاطعات مترابطة بشكل فضفاض

they had separate interests, laws, governments and systems of taxation

كان لديهم مصالح وقوانين وحكومات وأنظمة ضريبية منفصلة

but they have become lumped together into one nation, with one government

لكنهم أصبحوا مجتمعين معا في أمة واحدة ، مع حكومة واحدة

they now have one national class-interest, one frontier and one customs-tariff

لديهم الآن مصلحة طبقية وطنية واحدة ، وحدود واحدة ، وتعريفة جمركية واحدة

and this national class-interest is unified under one code of law

وهذه المصلحة الطبقية الوطنية موحدة تحت مدونة قانون واحدة

the Bourgeoisie has achieved much during its rule of scarce one hundred years

لقد حققت البرجوازية الكثير خلال حكمها النادر الذي دام مائة عام

more massive and colossal productive forces than have all preceding generations together

قوى إنتاجية أكثر ضخامة وهائلة من جميع الأجيال السابقة معا

Nature's forces are subjugated to the will of man and his machinery

تخضع قوى الطبيعة لإرادة الإنسان وآلياته

chemistry is applied to all forms of industry and types of agriculture

يتم تطبيق الكيمياء على جميع أشكال الصناعة وأنواع الزراعة

steam-navigation, railways, electric telegraphs, and the printing press

الملاحة البخارية والسكك الحديدية والتلغراف الكهربائي والمطبعة

clearing of whole continents for cultivation, canalisation of rivers

تطهير قارات بأكملها للزراعة ، وقنوات الأنهار

whole populations have been conjured out of the ground and put to work

لقد تم استحضار شعوب بأكملها من الأرض ووضعها في العمل

what earlier century had even a presentiment of what could be unleashed?

ما هو القرن السابق الذي كان لديه حتى شعور مسبق بما يمكن إطلاقه؟

who predicted that such productive forces slumbered in the lap of social labour?

من توقع أن مثل هذه القوى المنتجة سبات في حضن العمل الاجتماعي؟

we see then that the means of production and of exchange were generated in feudal society

نرى بعد ذلك أن وسائل الإنتاج والتبادل قد ولدت في المجتمع الإقطاعي

the means of production on whose foundation the Bourgeoisie built itself up

وسائل الإنتاج التي بنت البرجوازية نفسها على أساسها

At a certain stage in the development of these means of production and of exchange

في مرحلة معينة من تطور وسائل الإنتاج والتبادل هذه

the conditions under which feudal society produced and exchanged

الظروف التي أنتج فيها المجتمع الإقطاعي وتبادله

the feudal organisation of agriculture and manufacturing industry

التنظيم الإقطاعي للزراعة والصناعة التحويلية

the feudal relations of property were no longer compatible with the material conditions

لم تعد العلاقات الإقطاعية للملكية متوافقة مع الظروف المادية

They had to be burst asunder, so they were burst asunder

كان لا بد من انفجارهم ، لذلك تم تفجيرهم

Into their place stepped free competition from the productive forces

في مكانهم صعدت المنافسة الحرة من القوى المنتجة

and they were accompanied by a social and political constitution adapted to it

ورافقها دستور اجتماعي وسياسي يتكيف معها

and it was accompanied by the economical and political sway of the Bourgeoisie class

ورافقه النفوذ الاقتصادي والسياسي للطبقة البرجوازية.

A similar movement is going on before our own eyes

حركة مماثلة تجري أمام أعيننا

Modern Bourgeoisie society with its relations of production, and of exchange, and of property

المجتمع البرجوازي الحديث بعلاقات الإنتاج والتبادل والملكية

a society that has conjured up such gigantic means of production and of exchange

مجتمع استحضر مثل هذه الوسائل العملاقة للإنتاج والتبادل

it is like the sorcerer who called up the powers of the nether world

إنه مثل الساحر الذي استدعى قوى العالم السفلي

but he is no longer able to control what he has brought into the world

لكنه لم يعد قادرا على السيطرة على ما جلبه إلى العالم

For many a decade past history was tied together by a common thread

لعقد من الزمان ، كان التاريخ الماضي مرتبطا بخيط مشترك

the history of industry and commerce has been but the history of revolts

لم يكن تاريخ الصناعة والتجارة سوى تاريخ الثورات

the revolts of modern productive forces against modern conditions of production

ثورات القوى المنتجة الحديثة ضد ظروف الإنتاج الحديثة

the revolts of modern productive forces against property relations

ثورات القوى المنتجة الحديثة ضد علاقات الملكية

these property relations are the conditions for the existence of the Bourgeoisie

علاقات الملكية هذه هي شروط وجود البرجوازية

and the existence of the Bourgeoisie determines the rules for property relations

ووجود البرجوازية يحدد قواعد علاقات الملكية

it is enough to mention the periodical return of commercial crises

يكفي أن نذكر العودة الدورية للأزمات التجارية

each commercial crisis is more threatening to Bourgeoisie society than the last

كل أزمة تجارية تهدد المجتمع البرجوازي أكثر من سابقتها

In these crises a great part of the existing products are destroyed

في هذه الأزمات يتم تدمير جزء كبير من المنتجات الموجودة

but these crises also destroy the previously created productive forces

لكن هذه الأزمات تدمر أيضا القوى المنتجة التي تم إنشاؤها سابقا.

in all earlier epochs these epidemics would have seemed an absurdity

في جميع العصور السابقة ، كانت هذه الأوبئة تبدو سخيفة

because these epidemics are the commercial crises of over-production

لأن هذه الأوبئة هي الأزمات التجارية للإفراط في الإنتاج

Society suddenly finds itself put back into a state of momentary barbarism

يجد المجتمع نفسه فجأة في حالة من الهمجية اللحظية

as if a universal war of devastation had cut off every means of subsistence

كما لو أن حرب الدمار العالمية قد قطعت كل وسائل العيش

industry and commerce seem to have been destroyed; and why?

يبدو أن الصناعة والتجارة قد دمرت. ولماذا؟

Because there is too much civilisation and means of subsistence

لأن هناك الكثير من الحضارة ووسائل العيش

and because there is too much industry, and too much commerce

ولأن هناك الكثير من الصناعة ، والكثير من التجارة

The productive forces at the disposal of society no longer develop Bourgeoisie property

القوى المنتجة تحت تصرف المجتمع لم تعد تطور الملكية البرجوازية

on the contrary, they have become too powerful for these conditions, by which they are fettered

على العكس من ذلك ، فقد أصبحوا أقوياء للغاية بالنسبة لهذه الظروف ، التي يتم تقييدهم بها

as soon as they overcome these fetters, they bring disorder into the whole of Bourgeoisie society

بمجرد أن يتغلبوا على هذه القيود ، فإنهم يجلبون الفوضى إلى المجتمع البرجوازي بأكمله

and the productive forces endanger the existence of Bourgeoisie property

والقوى المنتجة تعرض للخطر وجود الملكية البرجوازية

The conditions of Bourgeoisie society are too narrow to comprise the wealth created by them

إن ظروف المجتمع البرجوازي أضيق من أن تشمل الثروة التي خلقوها.

And how does the Bourgeoisie get over these crises?

وكيف تتغلب البرجوازية على هذه الأزمات؟

On the one hand, it overcomes these crises by the enforced destruction of a mass of productive forces

فمن ناحية، تتغلب على هذه الأزمات من خلال التدمير القسري لكتلة من القوى المنتجة.

on the other hand, it overcomes these crises by the conquest of new markets

من ناحية أخرى ، فإنه يتغلب على هذه الأزمات من خلال غزو أسواق جديدة

and it overcomes these crises by the more thorough exploitation of the old forces of production

وتتغلب على هذه الأزمات من خلال الاستغلال الأكثر شمولا لقوى الإنتاج القديمة.

That is to say, by paving the way for more extensive and more destructive crises

وهذا يعني ، من خلال تمهيد الطريق لأزمات أكثر اتساعا وأكثر تدميرا.

it overcomes the crisis by diminishing the means whereby crises are prevented

إنه يتغلب على الأزمة من خلال تقليص الوسائل التي يتم من خلالها منع الأزمات

The weapons with which the Bourgeoisie felled feudalism to the ground are now turned against itself

إن الأسلحة التي أسقطت بها البرجوازية الإقطاع على الأرض تحولت الآن ضد نفسها

But not only has the Bourgeoisie forged the weapons that bring death to itself

لكن البرجوازية لم تقم فقط بصياغة الأسلحة التي تجلب الموت لنفسها

it has also called into existence the men who are to wield those weapons

كما دعت إلى الوجود الرجال الذين سيستخدمون تلك الأسلحة.

and these men are the modern working class; they are the proletarians

وهؤلاء الرجال هم الطبقة العاملة الحديثة. هم البروليتاريون

In proportion as the Bourgeoisie is developed, in the same proportion is the Proletariat developed

بالتناسب مع تطور البرجوازية ، بنفس النسبة تطورت البروليتاريا

the modern working class developed a class of labourers

طورت الطبقة العاملة الحديثة طبقة من العمال

this class of labourers live only so long as they find work

هذه الطبقة من العمال تعيش فقط طالما أنها تجد عملا

and they find work only so long as their labour increases capital

ويجدون عملا فقط طالما أن عملهم يزيد رأس المال

These labourers, who must sell themselves piece-meal, are a commodity

هؤلاء العمال، الذين يجب أن يبيعوا أنفسهم بالقطعة، هم سلعة.

these labourers are like every other article of commerce

هؤلاء العمال مثل أي مادة تجارية أخرى

and they are consequently exposed to all the vicissitudes of competition

وبالتالي يتعرضون لجميع تقلبات المنافسة

they have to weather all the fluctuations of the market

عليهم أن يتحملوا جميع تقلبات السوق

Owing to the extensive use of machinery and to division of labour

بسبب الاستخدام المكثف للآلات وتقسيم العمل

the work of the proletarians has lost all individual character

لقد فقد عمل البروليتاريين كل طابع فردي

and consequently, the work of the proletarians has lost all charm for the workman

وبالتالي ، فقد عمل البروليتاريين كل سحر للعامل

He becomes an appendage of the machine, rather than the man he once was

يصبح ملحقا للآلة ، بدلا من الرجل الذي كان عليه ذات مرة

only the most simple, monotonous, and most easily acquired knack is required of him

مطلوب منه فقط الموهبة الأكثر بساطة ورتابة والأكثر سهولة في الحصول عليها

Hence, the cost of production of a workman is restricted

وبالتالي ، فإن تكلفة إنتاج العامل مقيدة

it is restricted almost entirely to the means of subsistence that he requires for his maintenance

يقتصر بشكل شبه كامل على وسائل العيش التي يحتاجها لإعالته

and it is restricted to the means of subsistence that he requires for the propagation of his race

ويقتصر على وسائل العيش التي يحتاجها لنشر جنسه

But the price of a commodity, and therefore also of labour, is equal to its cost of production

لكن سعر السلعة ، وبالتالي أيضا العمل ، يساوي تكلفة إنتاجها.

In proportion, therefore, as the repulsiveness of the work increases, the wage decreases

بالتناسب ، لذلك ، مع زيادة تنافر العمل ، ينخفض الأجر

Nay, the repulsiveness of his work increases at an even greater rate

كلا ، يزداد اشمئزاز عمله بمعدل أكبر

as the use of machinery and division of labour increases, so does the burden of toil

مع زيادة استخدام الآلات وتقسيم العمل ، يزداد عبء الكدح

the burden of toil is increased by prolongation of the
working hours

يزداد عبء الكدح بإطالة ساعات العمل

more is expected of the labourer in the same time as before

يتوقع المزيد من العامل في نفس الوقت كما كان من قبل

and of course the burden of the toil is increased by the speed
of the machinery

وبالطبع يزداد عبء الكدح بسرعة الماكينة

Modern industry has converted the little workshop of the
patriarchal master into the great factory of the industrial
capitalist

لقد حولت الصناعة الحديثة الورشة الصغيرة للسيد البطريركي إلى مصنع
كبير للرأسمالي الصناعي

Masses of labourers, crowded into the factory, are organised
like soldiers

جماهير العمال، المحتشدة في المصنع، منظمة مثل الجنود

As privates of the industrial army they are placed under the
command of a perfect hierarchy of officers and sergeants

كجنود في الجيش الصناعي ، يتم وضعهم تحت قيادة تسلسل هرمي مثالي
من الضباط والرقباء

they are not only the slaves of the Bourgeoisie class and
State

إنهم ليسوا فقط عبيد الطبقة البرجوازية والدولة

but they are also daily and hourly enslaved by the machine

لكنهم أيضا مستعبدون يوميا وكل ساعة من قبل الآلة

they are enslaved by the over-looker, and, above all, by the
individual Bourgeoisie manufacturer himself

إنهم مستعبدون من قبل المتفرج ، وقبل كل شيء ، من قبل صانع
البرجوازية الفردي نفسه

The more openly this despotism proclaims gain to be its end
and aim, the more petty, the more hateful and the more
embittering it is

وكلما أعلن هذا الاستبداد بشكل علني أن المكاسب هي غايته وهدفه، كلما
كان أكثر تافهة، وأكثر بغضا وأكثر مرارة

the more modern industry becomes developed, the lesser are
the differences between the sexes

كلما تطورت الصناعة الحديثة ، قلت الاختلافات بين الجنسين

The less the skill and exertion of strength implied in manual labour, the more is the labour of men superseded by that of women

وكلما قلت مهارة وجهد القوة الذي ينطوي عليه العمل اليدوي، كلما حل عمل الرجال محل عمل النساء.

Differences of age and sex no longer have any distinctive social validity for the working class

لم يعد للاختلافات في العمر والجنس أي صلاحية اجتماعية مميزة للطبقة العاملة

All are instruments of labour, more or less expensive to use, according to their age and sex

وجميعها أدوات عمل، واستخدامها أكثر أو أقل تكلفة، وفقا لسنها وجنسها.

as soon as the labourer receives his wages in cash, than he is set upon by the other portions of the Bourgeoisie

بمجرد أن يتلقى العامل أجره نقدا ، يتم تحديده من قبل الأجزاء الأخرى من البرجوازية

the landlord, the shopkeeper, the pawnbroker, etc

المالك ، صاحب المتجر ، المرهن ، إلخ

The lower strata of the middle class; the small trades people and shopkeepers

الطبقات الدنيا من الطبقة الوسطى ؛ التجار الصغار وأصحاب المتاجر

the retired tradesmen generally, and the handicraftsmen and peasants

التجار المتقاعدون بشكل عام ، والحرفيون والفلاحون

all these sink gradually into the Proletariat

كل هذه تغرق تدريجيا في البروليتاريا

partly because their diminutive capital does not suffice for the scale on which Modern Industry is carried on

ويرجع ذلك جزئيا إلى أن رأس مالها الضئيل لا يكفي للنطاق الذي تتم فيه الصناعة الحديثة

and because it is swamped in the competition with the large capitalists

ولأنها غارقة في المنافسة مع كبار الرأسماليين

partly because their specialized skill is rendered worthless by the new methods of production

جزئيا لأن مهاراتهم المتخصصة أصبحت عديمة القيمة بسبب أساليب الإنتاج الجديدة

Thus the Proletariat is recruited from all classes of the population

وهكذا يتم تجنيد البروليتاريا من جميع طبقات السكان

The Proletariat goes through various stages of development

تمر البروليتاريا بمراحل مختلفة من التطور

With its birth begins its struggle with the Bourgeoisie

مع ولادتها يبدأ صراعها مع البرجوازية

At first the contest is carried on by individual labourers

في البداية يتم إجراء المسابقة من قبل العمال الأفراد

then the contest is carried on by the workpeople of a factory

ثم يتم إجراء المسابقة من قبل عمال المصنع

then the contest is carried on by the operatives of one trade, in one locality

ثم يتم إجراء المسابقة من قبل نشطاء تجارة واحدة ، في مكان واحد

and the contest is then against the individual Bourgeoisie who directly exploits them

والمنافسة إذن ضد البرجوازية الفردية التي تستغلها مباشرة

They direct their attacks not against the Bourgeoisie conditions of production

إنهم يوجهون هجماتهم ليس ضد ظروف الإنتاج البرجوازية

but they direct their attack against the instruments of production themselves

لكنهم يوجهون هجومهم ضد أدوات الإنتاج بأنفسهم.

they destroy imported wares that compete with their labour

إنهم يدمرون السلع المستوردة التي تنافس عملهم

they smash to pieces machinery and they set factories ablaze

لقد حطموا الآلات إلى قطع وأشعلوا النار في المصانع

they seek to restore by force the vanished status of the workman of the Middle Ages

إنهم يسعون إلى استعادة الوضع المختفي لعامل العصور الوسطى بالقوة

At this stage the labourers still form an incoherent mass scattered over the whole country

في هذه المرحلة لا يزال العمال يشكلون كتلة غير متماسكة منتشرة في جميع أنحاء البلاد.

and they are broken up by their mutual competition

ويتم تفكيكهم بسبب منافستهم المتبادلة

If anywhere they unite to form more compact bodies, this is not yet the consequence of their own active union

إذا اتحدوا في أي مكان لتشكيل هيئات أكثر إحكاما ، فهذا ليس نتيجة لاتحادهم النشط

but it is a consequence of the union of the Bourgeoisie, to attain its own political ends

لكنها نتيجة لاتحاد البرجوازية ، لتحقيق غاياتها السياسية الخاصة

the Bourgeoisie is compelled to set the whole Proletariat in motion

البرجوازية مجبرة على تحريك البروليتاريا بأكملها

and moreover, for a time being, the Bourgeoisie is able to do so

وعلاوة على ذلك ، في الوقت الحاضر ، فإن البرجوازية قادرة على القيام بذلك

At this stage, therefore, the proletarians do not fight their enemies

في هذه المرحلة ، لذلك ، لا يحارب البروليتاريون أعداءهم

but instead they are fighting the enemies of their enemies

لكنهم بدلا من ذلك يقاتلون أعداء أعدائهم.

the fight the remnants of absolute monarchy and the landowners

قتال فلول الملكية المطلقة وملاك الأراضي

they fight the non-industrial Bourgeoisie; the petty Bourgeoisie

إنهم يقاتلون البرجوازية غير الصناعية. البرجوازية الصغيرة

Thus the whole historical movement is concentrated in the hands of the Bourgeoisie

وهكذا تتركز الحركة التاريخية برمتها في أيدي البرجوازية

every victory so obtained is a victory for the Bourgeoisie

كل انتصار يتم الحصول عليه هو انتصار للبرجوازية

But with the development of industry the Proletariat not only increases in number

ولكن مع تطور الصناعة ، لا يزداد عدد البروليتاريا فقط

the Proletariat becomes concentrated in greater masses and its strength grows

تتركز البروليتاريا في كتل أكبر وتنمو قوتها

and the Proletariat feels that strength more and more

وتشعر البروليتاريا بهذه القوة أكثر فأكثر

The various interests and conditions of life within the ranks of the Proletariat are more and more equalised

إن المصالح والظروف المختلفة للحياة داخل صفوف البروليتاريا تتساوى أكثر فأكثر

they become more in proportion as machinery obliterates all distinctions of labour

تصبح أكثر تناسبا حيث تطمس الآلات جميع الفروق في العمل

and machinery nearly everywhere reduces wages to the same low level

والآلات في كل مكان تقريبا تخفض الأجور إلى نفس المستوى المنخفض

The growing competition among the Bourgeoisie, and the resulting commercial crises, make the wages of the workers ever more fluctuating

إن المنافسة المتزايدة بين البرجوازية، والأزمات التجارية الناتجة عنها، تجعل أجور العمال أكثر تقلبا من أي وقت مضى.

The unceasing improvement of machinery, ever more rapidly developing, makes their livelihood more and more precarious

إن التحسين المستمر للآلات ، الذي يتطور بسرعة أكبر من أي وقت مضى ، يجعل سبل عيشهم أكثر خطورة

the collisions between individual workmen and individual Bourgeoisie take more and more the character of collisions between two classes

تأخذ الاصطدامات بين العمال الأفراد والبرجوازية الفردية طابع الاصطدامات بين طبقتين أكثر فأكثر

Thereupon the workers begin to form combinations (Trades Unions) against the Bourgeoisie

عندها يبدأ العمال في تشكيل مجموعات (نقابات) ضد البرجوازية

they club together in order to keep up the rate of wages

إنهم يتعاونون معا من أجل الحفاظ على معدل الأجور

they found permanent associations in order to make
provision beforehand for these occasional revolts

لقد وجدوا جمعيات دائمة من أجل توفير هذه الثورات العرضية مسبقا

Here and there the contest breaks out into riots

هنا وهناك تندلع المسابقة في أعمال شغب

Now and then the workers are victorious, but only for a time

بين الحين والآخر ينتصر العمال ، ولكن فقط لبعض الوقت

The real fruit of their battles lies, not in the immediate
result, but in the ever-expanding union of the workers

إن الثمرة الحقيقية لمعاركهم لا تكمن في النتيجة الفورية، بل في اتحاد
العمال المتوسع باستمرار.

This union is helped on by the improved means of
communication that are created by modern industry

ويساعد هذا الاتحاد من خلال وسائل الاتصال المحسنة التي يتم إنشاؤها
بواسطة الصناعة الحديثة

modern communication places the workers of different
localities in contact with one another

الاتصالات الحديثة تضع العمال من مختلف المناطق على اتصال مع
بعضهم البعض

It was just this contact that was needed to centralise the
numerous local struggles into one national struggle between
classes

كان هذا الاتصال فقط هو المطلوب لتركيز النضالات المحلية العديدة في
صراع وطني واحد بين الطبقات.

all of these struggles are of the same character, and every
class struggle is a political struggle

كل هذه النضالات لها نفس الطابع ، وكل صراع طبقي هو صراع سياسي

the burghers of the Middle Ages, with their miserable
highways, required centuries to form their unions

احتاج البرغر في العصور الوسطى ، بطرقهم السريعة البائسة ، إلى قرون
لتشكيل نقاباتهم

the modern proletarians, thanks to railways, achieve their
unions within a few years

البروليتاريون الحديثون ، بفضل السكك الحديدية ، يحققون نقاباتهم في
غضون بضع سنوات

This organisation of the proletarians into a class consequently formed them into a political party

هذا التنظيم للبروليتاريين في طبقة شكلهم بالتالي في حزب سياسي

the political class is continually being upset again by the competition between the workers themselves

الطبقة السياسية مستاءة باستمرار مرة أخرى من المنافسة بين العمال أنفسهم

But the political class continues to rise up again, stronger, firmer, mightier

لكن الطبقة السياسية تستمر في النهوض مرة أخرى، أقوى وأكثر حزما وقوة.

It compels legislative recognition of particular interests of the workers

إنه يفرض الاعتراف التشريعي بالمصالح الخاصة للعمال

it does this by taking advantage of the divisions among the Bourgeoisie itself

وهي تفعل ذلك من خلال الاستفادة من الانقسامات بين البرجوازية نفسها

Thus the ten-hours' bill in England was put into law

وهكذا تم وضع مشروع قانون العشر ساعات في إنجلترا في القانون

in many ways the collisions between the classes of the old society further is the course of development of the Proletariat

من نواح كثيرة ، فإن الاصطدامات بين طبقات المجتمع القديم هي مسار تطور البروليتاريا

The Bourgeoisie finds itself involved in a constant battle

البرجوازية تجد نفسها متورطة في معركة مستمرة

At first it will find itself involved in a constant battle with the aristocracy

في البداية ستجد نفسها متورطة في معركة مستمرة مع الطبقة الأرستقراطية.

later on it will find itself involved in a constant battle with those portions of the Bourgeoisie itself

في وقت لاحق ستجد نفسها متورطة في معركة مستمرة مع تلك الأجزاء من البرجوازية نفسها

and their interests will have become antagonistic to the progress of industry

وستصبح مصالحهم معادية لتقدم الصناعة

at all times, their interests will have become antagonistic
with the Bourgeoisie of foreign countries

في جميع الأوقات ، ستصبح مصالحهم معادية لبرجوازية البلدان الأجنبية

In all these battles it sees itself compelled to appeal to the
Proletariat, and asks for its help

في كل هذه المعارك ترى نفسها مضطرة إلى مناشدة البروليتاريا ، وتطلب
مساعدتها

and thus, it will feel compelled to drag it into the political
arena

وبالتالي، ستشعر بأنها مضطرة لجرها إلى الساحة السياسية.

The Bourgeoisie itself, therefore, supplies the Proletariat
with its own instruments of political and general education

لذلك فإن البرجوازية نفسها تزود البروليتاريا بأدواتها الخاصة في التعليم
السياسي والعام.

in other words, it furnishes the Proletariat with weapons for
fighting the Bourgeoisie

وبعبارة أخرى، فإنه يزود البروليتاريا بالأسلحة لمحاربة البرجوازية.

Further, as we have already seen, entire sections of the
ruling classes are precipitated into the Proletariat

علاوة على ذلك ، كما رأينا بالفعل ، يتم ترسب قطاعات كاملة من الطبقات
الحاكمة في البروليتاريا

the advance of industry sucks them into the Proletariat

تقدم الصناعة يجذبهم إلى البروليتاريا

or, at least, they are threatened in their conditions of
existence

أو ، على الأقل ، هم مهددون في ظروف وجودهم

These also supply the Proletariat with fresh elements of
enlightenment and progress

هذه أيضا تزود البروليتاريا بعناصر جديدة من التنوير والتقدم

Finally, in times when the class struggle nears the decisive
hour

أخيرا ، في الأوقات التي يقترب فيها الصراع الطبقي من الساعة الحاسمة

the process of dissolution going on within the ruling class

عملية الانحلال الجارية داخل الطبقة الحاكمة

in fact, the dissolution going on within the ruling class will be felt within the whole range of society

في الواقع، إن الانحلال الذي يحدث داخل الطبقة الحاكمة سيكون محسوسا داخل كل نطاق المجتمع.

it will take on such a violent, glaring character, that a small section of the ruling class cuts itself adrift

سوف تتخذ طابعا عنيفا وصارخا ، بحيث يقطع قسم صغير من الطبقة الحاكمة نفسه على غير هدى.

and that ruling class will join the revolutionary class

وأن الطبقة الحاكمة ستنضم إلى الطبقة الثورية

the revolutionary class being the class that holds the future in its hands

الطبقة الثورية هي الطبقة التي تمسك بالمستقبل بين يديها

Just as at an earlier period, a section of the nobility went over to the Bourgeoisie

تماما كما في فترة سابقة ، ذهب قسم من النبلاء إلى البرجوازية

the same way a portion of the Bourgeoisie will go over to the Proletariat

بنفس الطريقة سيذهب جزء من البرجوازية إلى البروليتاريا

in particular, a portion of the Bourgeoisie will go over to a portion of the Bourgeoisie ideologists

على وجه الخصوص ، سيذهب جزء من البرجوازية إلى جزء من أيديولوجيات البرجوازية

Bourgeoisie ideologists who have raised themselves to the level of comprehending theoretically the historical movement as a whole

الإيديولوجيون البرجوازيون الذين رفعوا أنفسهم إلى مستوى الفهم النظري للحركة التاريخية ككل

Of all the classes that stand face to face with the Bourgeoisie today, the Proletariat alone is a really revolutionary class

من بين جميع الطبقات التي تقف وجها لوجه مع البرجوازية اليوم ، فإن البروليتاريا وحدها هي طبقة ثورية حقا

The other classes decay and finally disappear in the face of Modern Industry

الطبقات الأخرى تتحلل وتختفي أخيرا في مواجهة الصناعة الحديثة

the Proletariat is its special and essential product

البروليتاريا هي منتجها الخاص والأساسي

The lower middle class, the small manufacturer, the shopkeeper, the artisan, the peasant

الطبقة الوسطى الدنيا ، الشركة المصنعة الصغيرة ، صاحب المتجر ، الحرفي ، الفلاح

all these fight against the Bourgeoisie

كل هذه المعارك ضد البرجوازية

they fight as fractions of the middle class to save themselves from extinction

إنهم يقاتلون كأجزاء من الطبقة الوسطى لإنقاذ أنفسهم من الانقراض

They are therefore not revolutionary, but conservative

لذلك فهي ليست ثورية ، لكنها محافظة

Nay more, they are reactionary, for they try to roll back the wheel of history

لا أكثر، إنهم رجعيون، لأنهم يحاولون إعادة عجلة التاريخ إلى الوراء.

If by chance they are revolutionary, they are so only in view of their impending transfer into the Proletariat

إذا كانوا ثوريين بالصدفة ، فهم كذلك فقط في ضوء انتقالهم الوشيك إلى البروليتاريا

they thus defend not their present, but their future interests

وبالتالي فهم لا يدافعون عن حاضرهم ، بل عن مصالحهم المستقبلية

they desert their own standpoint to place themselves at that of the Proletariat

إنهم يتخلون عن وجهة نظرهم الخاصة ويضعون أنفسهم في موقف البروليتاريا

The "dangerous class," the social scum, that passively rotting mass thrown off by the lowest layers of old society

"الطبقة الخطرة" ، الحثالة الاجتماعية ، تلك الكتلة المتعفنة بشكل سلبي التي ألقيت بها الطبقات الدنيا من المجتمع القديم

they may, here and there, be swept into the movement by a proletarian revolution

قد تجتاحهم الثورة البروليتارية الحركة هنا وهناك.

its conditions of life, however, prepare it far more for the part of a bribed tool of reactionary intrigue

ومع ذلك ، فإن ظروف حياتها تعدها أكثر بكثير لجزء من أداة رشوة من المؤامرات الرجعية.

In the conditions of the Proletariat, those of old society at large are already virtually swamped

في ظروف البروليتاريا ، فإن ظروف المجتمع القديم ككل غارقة بالفعل في

The proletarian is without property

البروليتاري بلا ملكية

his relation to his wife and children has no longer anything in common with the Bourgeoisie's family-relations

علاقته بزوجته وأطفاله لم يعد لها أي شيء مشترك مع العلاقات الأسرية للبرجوازية

modern industrial labour, modern subjection to capital, the same in England as in France, in America as in Germany

العمل الصناعي الحديث ، والخضوع الحديث لرأس المال ، هو نفسه في إنجلترا كما في فرنسا ، في أمريكا كما في ألمانيا

his condition in society has stripped him of every trace of national character

حالته في المجتمع جردته من كل أثر للشخصية الوطنية

Law, morality, religion, are to him so many Bourgeoisie prejudices

القانون والأخلاق والدين ، هي بالنسبة له الكثير من التحيزات البرجوازية

and behind these prejudices lurk in ambush just as many Bourgeoisie interests

ووراء هذه التحيزات تكمن في كمين كما العديد من المصالح البرجوازية.

All the preceding classes that got the upper hand, sought to fortify their already acquired status

سعت جميع الطبقات السابقة التي كانت لها اليد العليا ، إلى تحصين وضعها المكتسب بالفعل

they did this by subjecting society at large to their conditions of appropriation

لقد فعلوا ذلك من خلال إخضاع المجتمع ككل لشروط الاستيلاء الخاصة بهم

The proletarians cannot become masters of the productive forces of society

لا يمكن للبروليتاريين أن يصبحوا سادة القوى المنتجة في المجتمع

it can only do this by abolishing their own previous mode of appropriation

لا يمكنها القيام بذلك إلا من خلال إلغاء طريقة التخصيص السابقة الخاصة بها

and thereby it also abolishes every other previous mode of appropriation

وبالتالي فإنه يلغي أيضا كل طريقة سابقة أخرى للتخصيص

They have nothing of their own to secure and to fortify

ليس لديهم شيء خاص بهم لتأمينه وتحصينه

their mission is to destroy all previous securities for, and insurances of, individual property

مهمتهم هي تدمير جميع الأوراق المالية السابقة للممتلكات الفردية وتأمينها

All previous historical movements were movements of minorities

جميع الحركات التاريخية السابقة كانت حركات أقليات

or they were movements in the interests of minorities

أو كانت حركات لصالح الأقليات

The proletarian movement is the self-conscious, independent movement of the immense majority

الحركة البروليتارية هي الحركة الواعية والمستقلة للأغلبية الساحقة

and it is a movement in the interests of the immense majority

وهي حركة تصب في مصلحة الأغلبية الساحقة

The Proletariat, the lowest stratum of our present society

البروليتاريا، أدنى طبقة في مجتمعنا الحالي

it cannot stir or raise itself up without the whole superincumbent strata of official society being sprung into the air

لا يمكنها أن تحرك أو ترفع نفسها دون أن تنتشر في الهواء الطبقات المتفوقة بأكملها في المجتمع الرسمي.

Though not in substance, yet in form, the struggle of the Proletariat with the Bourgeoisie is at first a national struggle

وإن لم يكن نضال البروليتاريا مع البرجوازية في الجوهر، إلا أنه في الشكل، هو في البداية نضال وطني.

The Proletariat of each country must, of course, first of all settle matters with its own Bourgeoisie

يجب على البروليتاريا في كل بلد ، بالطبع ، أولا وقبل كل شيء تسوية الأمور مع برجوازيتها الخاصة.

In depicting the most general phases of the development of the Proletariat, we traced the more or less veiled civil war

في تصوير المراحل الأكثر عمومية لتطور البروليتاريا ، تتبعنا الحرب الأهلية المبطنة إلى حد ما

this civil is raging within existing society

هذا المدني مستعر داخل المجتمع القائم

it will rage up to the point where that war breaks out into open revolution

سوف تحتدم إلى النقطة التي تندلع فيها تلك الحرب إلى ثورة مفتوحة

and then the violent overthrow of the Bourgeoisie lays the foundation for the sway of the Proletariat

ومن ثم فإن الإطاحة العنيفة بالبرجوازية تضع الأساس لسيطرة البروليتاريا

Hitherto, every form of society has been based, as we have already seen, on the antagonism of oppressing and oppressed classes

حتى الآن ، كان كل شكل من أشكال المجتمع قائما ، كما رأينا بالفعل ، على عداء الطبقات المضطهدة والمضطهدة

But in order to oppress a class, certain conditions must be assured to it

ولكن من أجل قمع الطبقة ، يجب ضمان شروط معينة لها

the class must be kept under conditions in which it can, at least, continue its slavish existence

يجب أن تبقى الطبقة في ظل ظروف يمكنها فيها ، على الأقل ، مواصلة وجودها العبودي

The serf, in the period of serfdom, raised himself to membership in the commune

رفع الأقنان ، في فترة القنانة ، نفسه إلى عضوية في البلدية

just as the petty Bourgeoisie, under the yoke of feudal absolutism, managed to develop into a Bourgeoisie

تماما كما تمكنت البرجوازية الصغيرة ، تحت نير الحكم المطلق الإقطاعي ، من التطور إلى برجوازية

The modern labourer, on the contrary, instead of rising with the progress of industry, sinks deeper and deeper

العامل الحديث ، على العكس من ذلك ، بدلا من النهوض مع تقدم الصناعة ، يغرق أعمق وأعمق

he sinks below the conditions of existence of his own class

يغرق تحت ظروف وجود طبقته

He becomes a pauper, and pauperism develops more rapidly than population and wealth

يصبح فقيرا ، ويتطور الفقر بسرعة أكبر من السكان والثروة

And here it becomes evident, that the Bourgeoisie is unfit any longer to be the ruling class in society

وهنا يصبح من الواضح أن البرجوازية لم تعد صالحة لتكون الطبقة الحاكمة في المجتمع

and it is unfit to impose its conditions of existence upon society as an over-riding law

ولا يصلح لفرض شروط وجوده على المجتمع كقانون مهيمن

It is unfit to rule because it is incompetent to assure an existence to its slave within his slavery

إنه غير صالح للحكم لأنه غير مؤهل لضمان وجود لعبده داخل عبوديته

because it cannot help letting him sink into such a state, that it has to feed him, instead of being fed by him

لأنه لا يمكن أن يساعد في السماح له بالغرق في مثل هذه الحالة ، بحيث يتعين عليه إطعامه ، بدلا من إطعامه من قبله

Society can no longer live under this Bourgeoisie

لم يعد بإمكان المجتمع العيش في ظل هذه البرجوازية

in other words, its existence is no longer compatible with society

بمعنى آخر ، لم يعد وجودها متوافقا مع المجتمع

The essential condition for the existence, and for the sway of the Bourgeoisie class, is the formation and augmentation of capital

إن الشرط الأساسي لوجود الطبقة البرجوازية وسيطرتها هو تكوين رأس المال وزيادته.

the condition for capital is wage-labour

شرط رأس المال هو العمل المأجور

Wage-labour rests exclusively on competition between the labourers

يعتمد العمل المأجور حصرا على المنافسة بين العمال

The advance of industry, whose involuntary promoter is the Bourgeoisie, replaces the isolation of the labourers

إن تقدم الصناعة، التي هي البرجوازية مروجها غير الطوعي، يحل محل عزلة العمال.

due to competition, due to their revolutionary combination, due to association

بسبب المنافسة ، بسبب مزيجهم الثوري ، بسبب الارتباط

The development of Modern Industry cuts from under its feet the very foundation on which the Bourgeoisie produces and appropriates products

إن تطور الصناعة الحديثة يقطع من تحت قدميه الأساس الذي تنتج عليه البرجوازية المنتجات وتستولي عليها.

What the Bourgeoisie produces, above all, is its own grave-diggers

ما تنتجه البرجوازية ، قبل كل شيء ، هو حفارو قبورها

The fall of the Bourgeoisie and the victory of the Proletariat are equally inevitable

إن سقوط البرجوازية وانتصار البروليتاريا أمر لا مفر منه بنفس القدر

Proletarians and Communists
البروليتاريون والشيوعيون

In what relation do the Communists stand to the proletarians as a whole?

في أي علاقة يقف الشيوعيون مع البروليتاريا ككل؟

The Communists do not form a separate party opposed to other working-class parties

لا يشكل الشيوعيون حزبا منفصلا يعارض أحزاب الطبقة العاملة الأخرى

They have no interests separate and apart from those of the proletariat as a whole

ليس لديهم مصالح منفصلة ومنفصلة عن مصالح البروليتاريا ككل.

They do not set up any sectarian principles of their own, by which to shape and mould the proletarian movement

إنهم لا يضعون أي مبادئ طائفية خاصة بهم ، لتشكيل وتشكيل الحركة البروليتارية

The Communists are distinguished from the other working-class parties by only two things

يتميز الشيوعيون عن أحزاب الطبقة العاملة الأخرى بأمرين فقط.

Firstly, they point out and bring to the front the common interests of the entire proletariat, independently of all nationality

أولا، إنهم يشيرون إلى المصالح المشتركة للبروليتاريا بأسرها، بغض النظر عن كل قومية.

this they do in the national struggles of the proletarians of the different countries

هذا ما يفعلونه في النضالات الوطنية للبروليتاريين في مختلف البلدان.

Secondly, they always and everywhere represent the interests of the movement as a whole

ثانيا، إنها تمثل دائما وفي كل مكان مصالح الحركة ككل.

this they do in the various stages of development, which the struggle of the working class against the Bourgeoisie has to pass through

هذا ما يفعلونه في مختلف مراحل التطور ، والتي يجب أن يمر بها نضال الطبقة العاملة ضد البرجوازية

The Communists, therefore, are on the one hand, practically, the most advanced and resolute section of the working-class parties of every country

لذلك فإن الشيوعيين هم من ناحية ، عمليا ، القسم الأكثر تقدما وتصميما من أحزاب الطبقة العاملة في كل بلد.

they are that section of the working class which pushes forward all others

إنهم ذلك القسم من الطبقة العاملة الذي يدفع جميع الآخرين إلى الأمام.

theoretically, they also have the advantage of clearly understanding the line of march

من الناحية النظرية ، لديهم أيضا ميزة فهم خط المسيرة بوضوح

this they understand better compared the great mass of the proletariat

هذا يفهمونه بشكل أفضل مقارنة بالكتلة العظمى للبروليتاريا

they understand the conditions, and the ultimate general results of the proletarian movement

إنهم يفهمون الظروف والنتائج العامة النهائية للحركة البروليتارية

The immediate aim of the Communist is the same as that of all the other proletarian parties

إن الهدف المباشر للشيوعية هو نفس هدف جميع الأحزاب البروليتارية الأخرى.

their aim is the formation of the proletariat into a class

هدفهم هو تشكيل البروليتاريا في طبقة

they aim to overthrow the Bourgeoisie supremacy

إنهم يهدفون إلى الإطاحة بسيادة البرجوازية

the strive for the conquest of political power by the proletariat

النضال من أجل الاستيلاء على السلطة السياسية من قبل البروليتاريا

The theoretical conclusions of the Communists are in no way based on ideas or principles of reformers

الاستنتاجات النظرية للشيوعيين لا تستند بأي حال من الأحوال إلى أفكار أو مبادئ الإصلاحيين

it wasn't would-be universal reformers that invented or discovered the theoretical conclusions of the Communists

لم يكن الإصلاحيون العالميون هم الذين اخترعوا أو اكتشفوا الاستنتاجات النظرية للشيوعيين

They merely express, in general terms, actual relations
springing from an existing class struggle

إنها تعبر فقط ، بعبارات عامة ، عن علاقات فعلية تنبع من صراع طبقي
قائم

and they describe the historical movement going on under
our very eyes that have created this class struggle

وهم يصفون الحركة التاريخية الجارية تحت أعيننا والتي خلقت هذا
الصراع الطبقي

The abolition of existing property relations is not at all a
distinctive feature of Communism

إن إلغاء علاقات الملكية القائمة ليس سمة مميزة للشيوعية على الإطلاق

All property relations in the past have continually been
subject to historical change

كانت جميع علاقات الملكية في الماضي تخضع باستمرار للتغيير التاريخي

and these changes were consequent upon the change in
historical conditions

وكانت هذه التغييرات نتيجة للتغير في الظروف التاريخية

The French Revolution, for example, abolished feudal
property in favour of Bourgeoisie property

الثورة الفرنسية ، على سبيل المثال ، ألغت الملكية الإقطاعية لصالح
الملكية البرجوازية

The distinguishing feature of Communism is not the
abolition of property, generally

السمة المميزة للشيوعية ليست إلغاء الملكية ، بشكل عام

but the distinguishing feature of Communism is the
abolition of Bourgeoisie property

لكن السمة المميزة للشيوعية هي إلغاء الملكية البرجوازية.

But modern Bourgeoisie private property is the final and
most complete expression of the system of producing and
appropriating products

لكن الملكية الخاصة البرجوازية الحديثة هي التعبير النهائي والأكثر اكتمالا
عن نظام إنتاج المنتجات والاستيلاء عليها.

it is the final state of a system that is based on class
antagonisms, where class antagonism is the exploitation of
the many by the few

إنها الحالة النهائية لنظام قائم على التناقضات الطبقية ، حيث العداء الطبقي هو استغلال الأكثرية من قبل القلة.

In this sense, the theory of the Communists may be summed up in the single sentence; the Abolition of private property

بهذا المعنى ، يمكن تلخيص نظرية الشيوعيين في جملة واحدة. إلغاء الملكية الخاصة

We Communists have been reproached with the desire of abolishing the right of personally acquiring property

لقد تم توبيخنا نحن الشيوعيين بالرغبة في إلغاء الحق في الحصول على الممتلكات شخصيا

it is claimed that this property is the fruit of a man's own labour

يزعم أن هذه الممتلكات هي ثمرة عمل الرجل نفسه

and this property is alleged to be the groundwork of all personal freedom, activity and independence.

ويزعم أن هذه الممتلكات هي أساس كل الحرية الشخصية والنشاط والاستقلال.

"Hard-won, self-acquired, self-earned property!"

"ممتلكات مكتسبة بشق الأنفس ، مكتسبة ذاتيا!"

Do you mean the property of the petty artisan and of the small peasant?

هل تقصد ممتلكات الحرفي الصغير والفلاح الصغير؟

Do you mean a form of property that preceded the Bourgeoisie form?

هل تقصد شكلا من أشكال الملكية التي سبقت شكل البرجوازية؟

There is no need to abolish that, the development of industry has to a great extent already destroyed it

ليست هناك حاجة لإلغاء ذلك ، فقد دمره تطوير الصناعة بالفعل إلى حد كبير

and development of industry is still destroying it daily

وتطور الصناعة مازال يدمرها يوميا

Or do you mean modern Bourgeoisie private property?

أم تقصد الملكية الخاصة البرجوازية الحديثة؟

But does wage-labour create any property for the labourer?

ولكن هل يخلق العمل المأجور أي ممتلكات للعامل؟

no, wage labour creates not one bit of this kind of property!

لا ، العمل المأجور لا يخلق جزءا واحدا من هذا النوع من الممتلكات!

what wage labour does create is capital; that kind of property which exploits wage-labour

ما يخلقه العمل المأجور هو رأس المال. هذا النوع من الممتلكات التي تستغل العمل المأجور

capital cannot increase except upon condition of begetting a new supply of wage-labour for fresh exploitation

لا يمكن لرأس المال أن يزيد إلا بشرط توليد عرض جديد من العمل المأجور لاستغلال جديد

Property, in its present form, is based on the antagonism of capital and wage-labour

تقوم الملكية، في شكلها الحالي، على عداء رأس المال والعمل المأجور

Let us examine both sides of this antagonism

دعونا نفحص كلا جانبي هذا العداء

To be a capitalist is to have not only a purely personal status

أن تكون رأسماليا لا يعني أن يكون لديك فقط حالة شخصية بحتة

instead, to be a capitalist is also to have a social status in production

بدلا من ذلك ، أن تكون رأسماليا هو أيضا أن يكون لديك وضع اجتماعي في الإنتاج

because capital is a collective product; only by the united action of many members can it be set in motion

لأن رأس المال هو منتج جماعي ؛ فقط من خلال العمل الموحد للعديد من الأعضاء يمكن تحريكه

but this united action is a last resort, and actually requires all members of society

لكن هذا العمل الموحد هو الملاذ الأخير ، ويتطلب في الواقع جميع أفراد المجتمع

Capital does get converted into the property of all members of society

يتم تحويل رأس المال إلى ملك لجميع أفراد المجتمع

but Capital is, therefore, not a personal power; it is a social power

لكن رأس المال ، إذن ، ليس قوة شخصية. إنها قوة اجتماعية

so when capital is converted into social property, personal property is not thereby transformed into social property

لذلك عندما يتم تحويل رأس المال إلى ملكية اجتماعية ، لا يتم تحويل الملكية الشخصية إلى ملكية اجتماعية

It is only the social character of the property that is changed, and loses its class-character

فقط الطابع الاجتماعي للممتلكات هو الذي يتغير ، ويفقد طابعه الطبقي

Let us now look at wage-labour

لنلق نظرة الآن على العمل المأجور

The average price of wage-labour is the minimum wage, i.e., that quantum of the means of subsistence

متوسط سعر العمل المأجور هو الحد الأدنى للأجور، أي مقدار وسائل العيش.

this wage is absolutely requisite in bare existence as a labourer

هذا الأجر مطلوب تماما في الوجود العاري كعامل

What, therefore, the wage-labourer appropriates by means of his labour, merely suffices to prolong and reproduce a bare existence

وبالتالي، فإن ما يستحوذ عليه العامل المأجور من خلال عمله، يكفي فقط لإطالة أمد وإعادة إنتاج وجود مجرد

We by no means intend to abolish this personal appropriation of the products of labour

نحن لا ننوي بأي حال من الأحوال إلغاء هذا الاستيلاء الشخصي على منتجات العمل

an appropriation that is made for the maintenance and reproduction of human life

اعتماد مخصص لصيانة الحياة البشرية وإعادة إنتاجها

such personal appropriation of the products of labour leave no surplus wherewith to command the labour of others

مثل هذا الاستيلاء الشخصي على منتجات العمل لا يترك فائضا لقيادة عمل الآخرين

All that we want to do away with, is the miserable character of this appropriation

كل ما نريد التخلص منه هو الطابع البائس لهذا الاستيلاء

the appropriation under which the labourer lives merely to increase capital

التخصيص الذي يعيش بموجبه العامل لمجرد زيادة رأس المال

he is allowed to live only in so far as the interest of the
ruling class requires it

لا يسمح له بالعيش إلا بقدر ما تقتضيه مصلحة الطبقة الحاكمة.

In Bourgeoisie society, living labour is but a means to
increase accumulated labour

في المجتمع البرجوازي، العمل الحي ليس سوى وسيلة لزيادة العمل المتراكم

In Communist society, accumulated labour is but a means to
widen, to enrich, to promote the existence of the labourer

في المجتمع الشيوعي، العمل المتراكم ليس سوى وسيلة لتوسيع وإثراء وتعزيز وجود العامل

In Bourgeoisie society, therefore, the past dominates the
present

في المجتمع البرجوازي، لذلك، يهيمن الماضي على الحاضر

in Communist society the present dominates the past

في المجتمع الشيوعي الحاضر يهيمن على الماضي

In Bourgeoisie society capital is independent and has
individuality

في المجتمع البرجوازي رأس المال مستقل وله فردية

In Bourgeoisie society the living person is dependent and
has no individuality

في المجتمع البرجوازي، يكون الشخص الحي تابعا وليس له فردية.

And the abolition of this state of things is called by the
Bourgeoisie, abolition of individuality and freedom!

وإلغاء هذه الحالة من الأشياء تسميه البرجوازية، إلغاء الفردية والحرية!

And it is rightly called the abolition of individuality and
freedom!

ويسمى بحق إلغاء الفردية والحرية!

Communism aims for the abolition of Bourgeoisie
individuality

الشيوعية تهدف إلى إلغاء الفردية البرجوازية

Communism intends for the abolition of Bourgeoisie
independence

الشيوعية تعتزم إلغاء استقلال البرجوازية

Bourgeoisie freedom is undoubtedly what communism is
aiming at

حرية البرجوازية هي بلا شك ما تهدف إليه الشيوعية

under the present Bourgeoisie conditions of production, freedom means free trade, free selling and buying

في ظل ظروف الإنتاج البرجوازية الحالية ، تعني الحرية التجارة الحرة والبيع والشراء الحر

But if selling and buying disappears, free selling and buying also disappears

اما اذا اختفى البيع والشراء اختفى البيع والشراء الحر ايضا

"brave words" by the Bourgeoisie about free selling and buying only have meaning in a limited sense

"الكلمات الشجاعة" من قبل البرجوازية حول البيع والشراء الحر لها معنى محدود فقط

these words have meaning only in contrast with restricted selling and buying

هذه الكلمات لها معنى فقط على عكس البيع والشراء المقيد.

and these words have meaning only when applied to the fettered traders of the Middle Ages

وهذه الكلمات لها معنى فقط عند تطبيقها على التجار المقيدين في العصور الوسطى

and that assumes these words even have meaning in a Bourgeoisie sense

وهذا يفترض أن هذه الكلمات لها معنى بالمعنى البرجوازي

but these words have no meaning when they're being used to oppose the Communistic abolition of buying and selling

لكن هذه الكلمات ليس لها معنى عندما يتم استخدامها لمعارضة الإلغاء الشيوعي للشراء والبيع

the words have no meaning when they're being used to oppose the Bourgeoisie conditions of production being abolished

الكلمات ليس لها معنى عندما يتم استخدامها لمعارضة إلغاء شروط الإنتاج البرجوازية

and they have no meaning when they're being used to oppose the Bourgeoisie itself being abolished

وليس لها أي معنى عندما يتم استخدامها لمعارضة إلغاء البرجوازية نفسها

You are horrified at our intending to do away with private property

أنت مرعوب من نيتنا التخلص من الممتلكات الخاصة

But in your existing society, private property is already done
away with for nine-tenths of the population

ولكن في مجتمعك الحالي ، تم بالفعل التخلص من الملكية الخاصة لتسعة
أعشار السكان

the existence of private property for the few is solely due to
its non-existence in the hands of nine-tenths of the
population

إن وجود الملكية الخاصة للقلة يرجع فقط إلى عدم وجودها في أيدي تسعة
أعشار السكان

You reproach us, therefore, with intending to do away with a
form of property

أنت تلومنا ، لذلك ، بنية التخلص من شكل من أشكال الملكية

but private property necessitates the non-existence of any
property for the immense majority of society

لكن الملكية الخاصة تستلزم عدم وجود أي ممتلكات للغالبية العظمى من
المجتمع

In one word, you reproach us with intending to do away
with your property

بكلمة واحدة ، أنت تلومنا على نية التخلص من ممتلكاتك

And it is precisely so; doing away with your Property is just
what we intend

وهذا هو بالضبط كذلك. التخلص من الممتلكات الخاصة بك هو بالضبط ما
نعتزم

From the moment when labour can no longer be converted
into capital, money, or rent

من اللحظة التي لم يعد من الممكن فيها تحويل العمل إلى رأس مال أو مال
أو إيجار

when labour can no longer be converted into a social power
capable of being monopolised

عندما لا يعود من الممكن تحويل العمل إلى قوة اجتماعية قادرة على
الاحتكار

from the moment when individual property can no longer
be transformed into Bourgeoisie property

من اللحظة التي لم يعد من الممكن فيها تحويل الملكية الفردية إلى ملكية
برجوازية

from the moment when individual property can no longer be transformed into capital

من اللحظة التي لم يعد من الممكن فيها تحويل الملكية الفردية إلى رأس مال

from that moment, you say individuality vanishes

من تلك اللحظة ، تقول إن الفردية تختفي

You must, therefore, confess that by "individual" you mean no other person than the Bourgeoisie

لذلك يجب أن تعترف بأنك لا تعني بكلمة "فرد" أي شخص آخر غير البرجوازية.

you must confess it specifically refers to the middle-class owner of property

يجب أن تعترف أنه يشير على وجه التحديد إلى مالك العقار من الطبقة الوسطى

This person must, indeed, be swept out of the way, and made impossible

يجب بالفعل أن يجرف هذا الشخص بعيدا عن الطريق ، ويصبح مستحيلا

Communism deprives no man of the power to appropriate the products of society

الشيوعية لا تحرم أي إنسان من القدرة على الاستيلاء على منتجات المجتمع

all that Communism does is to deprive him of the power to subjugate the labour of others by means of such appropriation

كل ما تفعله الشيوعية هو حرمانه من القدرة على إخضاع عمل الآخرين عن طريق هذا الاستيلاء

It has been objected that upon the abolition of private property all work will cease

وقد اعترض على أنه عند إلغاء الملكية الخاصة ستتوقف جميع الأعمال

and it is then suggested that universal laziness will overtake us

ثم يقترح أن الكسل العالمي سوف يتفوق علينا

According to this, Bourgeoisie society ought long ago to have gone to the dogs through sheer idleness

وفقا لهذا ، كان يجب على المجتمع البرجوازي منذ فترة طويلة أن يذهب إلى من خلال الكسل المطلق

because those of its members who work, acquire nothing

لأن أولئك الذين يعملون من أعضائها ، لا يكتسبون شيئا

and those of its members who acquire anything, do not work

وأولئك من أعضائها الذين يحصلون على أي شيء ، لا يعملون

The whole of this objection is but another expression of the tautology

كل هذا الاعتراض ليس سوى تعبير آخر عن الحشو

there can no longer be any wage-labour when there is no longer any capital

لا يمكن أن يكون هناك أي عمل مأجور عندما لا يكون هناك أي رأس مال

there is no difference between material products and mental products

لا يوجد فرق بين المنتجات المادية والمنتجات العقلية

communism proposes both of these are produced in the same way

تقترح الشيوعية أن يتم إنتاج كلاهما بنفس الطريقة

but the objections against the Communistic modes of producing these are the same

لكن الاعتراضات ضد الأنماط الشيوعية لإنتاج هذه هي نفسها

to the Bourgeoisie the disappearance of class property is the disappearance of production itself

بالنسبة للبرجوازية ، فإن اختفاء الملكية الطبقية هو اختفاء الإنتاج نفسه

so the disappearance of class culture is to him identical with the disappearance of all culture

لذا فإن اختفاء الثقافة الطبقية بالنسبة له مطابق لاختفاء كل ثقافة

That culture, the loss of which he laments, is for the enormous majority a mere training to act as a machine

هذه الثقافة ، التي يأسف لفقدانها ، هي بالنسبة للغالبية العظمى مجرد تدريب للعمل كآلة

Communists very much intend to abolish the culture of Bourgeoisie property

يعتزم الشيوعيون بشدة إلغاء ثقافة الملكية البرجوازية

But don't wrangle with us so long as you apply the standard of your Bourgeoisie notions of freedom, culture, law, etc

لكن لا تتجادلوا معنا طالما أنكم تطبقون معيار مفاهيمكم البرجوازية عن الحرية والثقافة والقانون وما إلى ذلك.

Your very ideas are but the outgrowth of the conditions of your Bourgeoisie production and Bourgeoisie property

إن أفكاركم ذاتها ليست سوى نتاج ظروف إنتاجكم البرجوازي وممتلكاتكم البرجوازية

just as your jurisprudence is but the will of your class made into a law for all

كما أن اجتهادكم ما هو إلا إرادة طبقتكم التي تحولت إلى قانون للجميع

the essential character and direction of this will are determined by the economical conditions your social class create

يتم تحديد الطابع الأساسي واتجاه هذه الإرادة من خلال الظروف الاقتصادية التي تخلقها طبقتك الاجتماعية

The selfish misconception that induces you to transform social forms into eternal laws of nature and of reason

المفهوم الخاطئ الأناني الذي يدفعك إلى تحويل الأشكال الاجتماعية إلى قوانين أبدية للطبيعة والعقل

the social forms springing from your present mode of production and form of property

الأشكال الاجتماعية المنبثقة من نمط الإنتاج الحالي وشكل الملكية

historical relations that rise and disappear in the progress of production

العلاقات التاريخية التي ترتفع وتختفي في تقدم الإنتاج

this misconception you share with every ruling class that has preceded you

هذا المفهوم الخاطئ الذي تشاركه مع كل طبقة حاكمة سبقتك

What you see clearly in the case of ancient property, what you admit in the case of feudal property

ما تراه بوضوح في حالة الملكية القديمة ، ما تعترف به في حالة الملكية الإقطاعية

these things you are of course forbidden to admit in the case of your own Bourgeoisie form of property

هذه الأشياء ممنوع عليك بالطبع الاعتراف بها في حالة شكل الملكية البرجوازية الخاص بك

Abolition of the family! Even the most radical flare up at this infamous proposal of the Communists

إلغاء الأسرة! حتى أكثر الراديكالية اشتعال في هذا الاقتراح سيئ السمعة للشيوعيين

On what foundation is the present family, the Bourgeoisie family, based?

على أي أساس تقوم الأسرة الحالية ، عائلة البرجوازية؟

the foundation of the present family is based on capital and private gain

يعتمد أساس الأسرة الحالية على رأس المال والمكاسب الخاصة

In its completely developed form this family exists only among the Bourgeoisie

في شكلها المتطور تماما ، هذه العائلة موجودة فقط بين البرجوازية

this state of things finds its complement in the practical absence of the family among the proletarians

هذه الحالة من الأشياء تجد تكملتها في الغياب العملي للعائلة بين البروليتاريين.

this state of things can be found in public prostitution

يمكن العثور على هذه الحالة من الأشياء في الدعارة العامة

The Bourgeoisie family will vanish as a matter of course when its complement vanishes

ستختفي العائلة البرجوازية بطبيعة الحال عندما يختفي مكملتها

and both of these will will vanish with the vanishing of capital

وكلاهما سوف يختفي مع تلاشي رأس المال

Do you charge us with wanting to stop the exploitation of children by their parents?

هل تتهموننا بالرغبة في وقف استغلال الأطفال من قبل والديهم؟

To this crime we plead guilty

نعترف بالذنب في هذه الجريمة

But, you will say, we destroy the most hallowed of relations, when we replace home education by social education

ولكن، كما ستقولون، نحن ندمر أقدس العلاقات، عندما نستبدل التعليم المنزلي بالتعليم الاجتماعي.

is your education not also social? And is it not determined by the social conditions under which you educate?

أليس تعليمك اجتماعيا أيضا؟ وألا تحدده الظروف الاجتماعية التي تتعلمون في ظلها؟

by the intervention, direct or indirect, of society, by means
of schools, etc.

من خلال التدخل المباشر أو غير المباشر للمجتمع ، عن طريق المدارس ،
إلخ.

The Communists have not invented the intervention of
society in education

الشيوعيون لم يخترعوا تدخل المجتمع في التعليم

they do but seek to alter the character of that intervention

إنهم يفعلون ذلك لكنهم يسعون إلى تغيير طابع هذا التدخل

and they seek to rescue education from the influence of the
ruling class

ويسعون إلى إنقاذ التعليم من تأثير الطبقة الحاكمة

The Bourgeoisie talk of the hallowed co-relation of parent
and child

تتحدث البرجوازية عن العلاقة المشتركة المقدسة بين الوالدين والطفل

but this clap-trap about the family and education becomes
all the more disgusting when we look at Modern Industry

لكن فخ التصفيق هذا حول الأسرة والتعليم يصبح أكثر إثارة للاشمئزاز
عندما ننظر إلى الصناعة الحديثة

all family ties among the proletarians are torn asunder by
modern industry

تمزق جميع الروابط الأسرية بين البروليتاريين بسبب الصناعة الحديثة

their children are transformed into simple articles of
commerce and instruments of labour

يتم تحويل أطفالهم إلى مواد تجارية بسيطة وأدوات عمل

But you Communists would create a community of women,
screams the whole Bourgeoisie in chorus

لكنكم أيها الشيوعيون ستخلقون مجتمعا من النساء ، تصرخ البرجوازية
بأكملها في جوقة

The Bourgeoisie sees in his wife a mere instrument of
production

يرى البرجوازي في زوجته مجرد أداة للإنتاج

He hears that the instruments of production are to be
exploited by all

يسمع أن أدوات الإنتاج يجب أن يستغلها الجميع

and, naturally, he can come to no other conclusion than that the lot of being common to all will likewise fall to women

وبطبيعة الحال ، لا يمكنه التوصل إلى أي استنتاج آخر سوى أن الكثير من القواسم المشتركة بين الجميع ستقع بالمثل على النساء.

He has not even a suspicion that the real point is to do away with the status of women as mere instruments of production

ليس لديه حتى شك في أن الهدف الحقيقي هو التخلص من وضع المرأة كمجرد أدوات للإنتاج.

For the rest, nothing is more ridiculous than the virtuous indignation of our Bourgeoisie at the community of women

بالنسبة للبقية، ليس هناك ما هو أكثر سخافة من السخط الفاضل لبرجوازيتنا على مجتمع النساء.

they pretend it is to be openly and officially established by the Communists

يتظاهرون بأنه سيتم تأسيسها بشكل علني ورسمي من قبل الشيوعيين

The Communists have no need to introduce community of women, it has existed almost from time immemorial

الشيوعيون ليسوا بحاجة إلى إدخال مجتمع من النساء ، فقد كان موجودا منذ زمن سحيق تقريبا

Our Bourgeoisie are not content with having the wives and daughters of their proletarians at their disposal

إن برجوازيتنا لا تكتفي بوجود زوجات وبنات البروليتاريين تحت تصرفها.

they take the greatest pleasure in seducing each other's wives

يأخذون أكبر متعة في إغواء زوجات بعضهم البعض

and that is not even to speak of common prostitutes

وهذا لا يعني حتى الحديث عن البغايا العاديات

Bourgeoisie marriage is in reality a system of wives in common

الزواج البرجوازي هو في الواقع نظام زوجات مشترك

then there is one thing that the Communists might possibly be reproached with

ثم هناك شيء واحد يمكن أن يلوم الشيوعيين عليه

they desire to introduce an openly legalised community of women

إنهم يرغبون في تقديم مجتمع نسائي قانوني بشكل علني

rather than a hypocritically concealed community of women

بدلا من مجتمع نسائي مخفي بشكل منافق

the community of women springing from the system of production

مجتمع المرأة المنبثق من نظام الإنتاج

abolish the system of production, and you abolish the community of women

ألغوا نظام الإنتاج، وأنتم تلغون مجتمع النساء

both public prostitution is abolished, and private prostitution

إلغاء كل من الدعارة العامة والدعارة الخاصة

The Communists are further more reproached with desiring to abolish countries and nationality

الشيوعيون أكثر لوما على رغبتهم في إلغاء البلدان والقومية.

The working men have no country, so we cannot take from them what they have not got

العمال ليس لديهم وطن، لذلك لا يمكننا أن نأخذ منهم ما لم يحصلوا عليه

the proletariat must first of all acquire political supremacy

يجب على البروليتاريا أولا وقبل كل شيء الحصول على السيادة السياسية

the proletariat must rise to be the leading class of the nation

يجب أن تنهض البروليتاريا لتكون الطبقة الرائدة في الأمة

the proletariat must constitute itself the nation

يجب أن تشكل البروليتاريا نفسها الأمة

it is, so far, itself national, though not in the Bourgeoisie sense of the word

إنها ، حتى الآن ، وطنية ، وإن لم يكن بالمعنى البرجوازي للكلمة

National differences and antagonisms between peoples are daily more and more vanishing

الخلافات والعداوات الوطنية بين الشعوب تتلاشى يوميا أكثر فأكثر

owing to the development of the Bourgeoisie, to freedom of commerce, to the world-market

بسبب تطور البرجوازية ، وحرية التجارة ، والسوق العالمية

to uniformity in the mode of production and in the conditions of life corresponding thereto

إلى التوحيد في نمط الإنتاج وفي ظروف الحياة المقابلة له

The supremacy of the proletariat will cause them to vanish
still faster

سيادة البروليتاريا ستؤدي إلى اختفائها بشكل أسرع

United action, of the leading civilised countries at least, is
one of the first conditions for the emancipation of the
proletariat

إن العمل الموحد، للبلدان المتحضرة الرائدة على الأقل، هو أحد الشروط
الأولى لتحرير البروليتاريا.

In proportion as the exploitation of one individual by
another is put an end to, the exploitation of one nation by
another will also be put an end to

بالتناسب مع وضع حد لاستغلال فرد من قبل شخص آخر ، فإن استغلال
أمة من قبل دولة أخرى سيتم أيضا وضع حد له

In proportion as the antagonism between classes within the
nation vanishes, the hostility of one nation to another will
come to an end

بالتناسب مع تلاشي العداء بين الطبقات داخل الأمة ، سينتهي عداء أمة
لأخرى

The charges against Communism made from a religious, a
philosophical, and, generally, from an ideological
standpoint, are not deserving of serious examination

إن التهم الموجهة ضد الشيوعية من وجهة نظر دينية وفلسفية ، وبشكل
عام من وجهة نظر أيديولوجية ، لا تستحق فحصا جادا

Does it require deep intuition to comprehend that man's
ideas, views and conceptions changes with every change in
the conditions of his material existence?

هل يتطلب الأمر حدسا عميقا لفهم أن أفكار الإنسان وآرائه وتصوراته
تتغير مع كل تغيير في ظروف وجوده المادي؟

is it not obvious that man's consciousness changes when his
social relations and his social life changes?

أليس من الواضح أن وعي الإنسان يتغير عندما تتغير علاقاته الاجتماعية
وحياته الاجتماعية؟

What else does the history of ideas prove, than that
intellectual production changes its character in proportion as
material production is changed?

ماذا يثبت تاريخ الأفكار ، غير أن الإنتاج الفكري يغير طابعه بالتناسب مع تغير الإنتاج المادي؟

The ruling ideas of each age have ever been the ideas of its ruling class

الأفكار الحاكمة في كل عصر كانت أفكار الطبقة الحاكمة

When people speak of ideas that revolutionise society, they do but express one fact

عندما يتحدث الناس عن الأفكار التي تحدث ثورة في المجتمع ، فإنهم يفعلون ذلك ولكنهم يعبرون عن حقيقة واحدة

within the old society, the elements of a new one have been created

داخل المجتمع القديم ، تم إنشاء عناصر مجتمع جديد

and that the dissolution of the old ideas keeps even pace with the dissolution of the old conditions of existence

وأن انحلال الأفكار القديمة يواكب انحلال الظروف القديمة للوجود

When the ancient world was in its last throes, the ancient religions were overcome by Christianity

عندما كان العالم القديم في مخاضه الأخير ، تغلبت المسيحية على الأديان القديمة

When Christian ideas succumbed in the 18th century to rationalist ideas, feudal society fought its death battle with the then revolutionary Bourgeoisie

عندما استسلمت الأفكار المسيحية في القرن 18 للأفكار العقلانية ، خاض المجتمع الإقطاعي معركة الموت مع البرجوازية الثورية آنذاك

The ideas of religious liberty and freedom of conscience merely gave expression to the sway of free competition within the domain of knowledge

إن أفكار الحرية الدينية وحرية الضمير لم تعبر إلا عن تأثير المنافسة الحرة في مجال المعرفة.

"Undoubtedly," it will be said, "religious, moral, philosophical and juridical ideas have been modified in the course of historical development"

"مما لا شك فيه أن الأفكار الدينية والأخلاقية والفلسفية والقانونية قد تم تعديلها في سياق التطور التاريخي"

"But religion, morality philosophy, political science, and law, constantly survived this change"

"لكن الدين وفلسفة الأخلاق والعلوم السياسية والقانون نجت باستمرار من هذا التغيير"

"There are also eternal truths, such as Freedom, Justice, etc"

"هناك أيضا حقائق أبدية ، مثل الحرية والعدالة وما إلى ذلك"

"these eternal truths are common to all states of society"

"هذه الحقائق الأبدية مشتركة بين جميع حالات المجتمع"

"But Communism abolishes eternal truths, it abolishes all religion, and all morality"

"لكن الشيوعية تلغي الحقائق الأبدية ، وتلغي كل الدين ، وكل الأخلاق"

"it does this instead of constituting them on a new basis"

"إنها تفعل ذلك بدلا من تشكيلها على أساس جديد"

"it therefore acts in contradiction to all past historical experience"

"لذلك فهو يتناقض مع كل التجارب التاريخية الماضية"

What does this accusation reduce itself to?

إلى ماذا يختزل هذا الاتهام؟

The history of all past society has consisted in the development of class antagonisms

تألف تاريخ كل المجتمع الماضي في تطور العداوات الطبقية.

antagonisms that assumed different forms at different epochs

التناقضات التي اتخذت أشكالا مختلفة في عصور مختلفة

But whatever form they may have taken, one fact is common to all past ages

ولكن مهما كان الشكل الذي اتخذوه ، هناك حقيقة واحدة مشتركة بين جميع العصور الماضية

the exploitation of one part of society by the other

استغلال جزء من المجتمع من قبل الآخر

No wonder, then, that the social consciousness of past ages moves within certain common forms, or general ideas

لا عجب إذن أن يتحرك الوعي الاجتماعي في العصور الماضية ضمن أشكال مشتركة معينة ، أو أفكار عامة.

(and that is despite all the multiplicity and variety it displays)

(وهذا على الرغم من كل التعدد والتنوع الذي يعرضه)

and these cannot completely vanish except with the total
disappearance of class antagonisms

ولا يمكن أن تختفي هذه تماما إلا مع الاختفاء التام للعداوات الطبقية.

The Communist revolution is the most radical rupture with
traditional property relations

الثورة الشيوعية هي القطيعة الأكثر جذرية مع علاقات الملكية التقليدية

no wonder that its development involves the most radical
rupture with traditional ideas

لا عجب أن تطورها ينطوي على تمزق جذري مع الأفكار التقليدية.

But let us have done with the Bourgeoisie objections to
Communism

لكن دعونا نفعل مع اعتراضات البرجوازية على الشيوعية

We have seen above the first step in the revolution by the
working class

لقد رأينا أعلاه الخطوة الأولى في الثورة من قبل الطبقة العاملة

proletariat has to be raised to the position of ruling, to win
the battle of democracy

يجب رفع البروليتاريا إلى موقع الحكم، لكسب معركة الديمقراطية.

The proletariat will use its political supremacy to wrest, by
degrees, all capital from the Bourgeoisie

ستستخدم البروليتاريا تفوقها السياسي لانتزاع كل رأس المال من
البرجوازية بدرجات.

it will centralise all instruments of production in the hands
of the State

ستركز جميع أدوات الإنتاج في أيدي الدولة

in other words, the proletariat organised as the ruling class

وبعبارة أخرى، نظمت البروليتاريا كطبقة حاكمة

and it will increase the total of productive forces as rapidly
as possible

وسيزيد من مجموع القوى المنتجة في أسرع وقت ممكن

Of course, in the beginning, this cannot be effected except
by means of despotic inroads on the rights of property

بالطبع ، في البداية ، لا يمكن تحقيق ذلك إلا عن طريق الاختراقات
الاستبدادية لحقوق الملكية

and it has to be achieved on the conditions of Bourgeoisie
production

ويجب أن يتحقق ذلك وفقا لظروف الإنتاج البرجوازي

it is achieved by means of measures, therefore, which appear economically insufficient and untenable

يتم تحقيقه عن طريق التدابير ، وبالتالي ، والتي تبدو غير كافية اقتصاديا ولا يمكن الدفاع عنها.

but these means, in the course of the movement, outstrip themselves

لكن هذه الوسائل ، في سياق الحركة ، تفوق نفسها

they necessitate further inroads upon the old social order

إنها تتطلب المزيد من الاختراقات على النظام الاجتماعي القديم

and they are unavoidable as a means of entirely revolutionising the mode of production

وهي لا مفر منها كوسيلة لإحداث ثورة كاملة في نمط الإنتاج

These measures will of course be different in different countries

ستكون هذه التدابير بالطبع مختلفة في مختلف البلدان

Nevertheless in the most advanced countries, the following will be pretty generally applicable

ومع ذلك ، في البلدان الأكثر تقدما ، سيكون ما يلي قابلا للتطبيق بشكل عام

1. Abolition of property in land and application of all rents of land to public purposes.

1. إلغاء الملكية في الأراضي وتطبيق جميع إيجارات الأراضي للأغراض العامة.

2. A heavy progressive or graduated income tax.

2. ضريبة دخل تصاعدية أو متدرجة ثقيلة.

3. Abolition of all right of inheritance.

3. إلغاء جميع حقوق الميراث.

4. Confiscation of the property of all emigrants and rebels.

4. مصادرة ممتلكات جميع المهاجرين والمتمردين.

5. Centralisation of credit in the hands of the State, by means of a national bank with State capital and an exclusive monopoly.

5. مركزية الائتمان في يد الدولة، عن طريق بنك وطني برأس مال الدولة واحتكار حصري.

6. Centralisation of the means of communication and transport in the hands of the State.

.6- مركزية وسائل الاتصال والنقل في يد الدولة

7. Extension of factories and instruments of production owned by the State

7- توسعة المصانع وأدوات الإنتاج المملوكة للدولة

the bringing into cultivation of waste-lands, and the improvement of the soil generally in accordance with a common plan.

جلب الأراضي البور إلى الزراعة ، وتحسين التربة بشكل عام وفقا لخطة
مشتركة.

8. Equal liability of all to labour

8. المسؤولية المتساوية للجميع عن العمل

Establishment of industrial armies, especially for agriculture.

إنشاء الجيوش الصناعية ، وخاصة للزراعة.

9. Combination of agriculture with manufacturing industries

9. مزيج من الزراعة مع الصناعات التحويلية

gradual abolition of the distinction between town and country, by a more equable distribution of the population over the country.

الإلغاء التدريجي للتمييز بين المدينة والريف ، من خلال توزيع أكثر
مساواة للسكان في جميع أنحاء البلاد.

10. Free education for all children in public schools.

10. التعليم المجاني لجميع الأطفال في المدارس العامة.

Abolition of children's factory labour in its present form

إلغاء عمل الأطفال في المصانع بشكله الحالي

Combination of education with industrial production

مزيج من التعليم مع الإنتاج الصناعي

When, in the course of development, class distinctions have disappeared

عندما تختفي الفروق الطبقية في سياق التطور

and when all production has been concentrated in the hands of a vast association of the whole nation

وعندما يتركز كل الإنتاج في أيدي جمعية واسعة من الأمة كلها

then the public power will lose its political character

عندها ستفقد السلطة العامة طابعها السياسي

Political power, properly so called, is merely the organised power of one class for oppressing another

السلطة السياسية ، التي تسمى بشكل صحيح ، هي مجرد قوة منظمة لطبقة واحدة لقمع طبقة أخرى

If the proletariat during its contest with the Bourgeoisie is compelled, by the force of circumstances, to organise itself as a class

إذا اضطرت البروليتاريا خلال صراعها مع البرجوازية ، بقوة الظروف ، إلى تنظيم نفسها كطبقة

if, by means of a revolution, it makes itself the ruling class

إذا، عن طريق الثورة، جعلت نفسها الطبقة الحاكمة

and, as such, it sweeps away by force the old conditions of production

وعلى هذا النحو ، فإنه يجرف بالقوة ظروف الإنتاج القديمة

then it will, along with these conditions, have swept away the conditions for the existence of class antagonisms and of classes generally

عندها ، إلى جانب هذه الظروف ، قد جرفت شروط وجود التناقضات الطبقية والطبقات بشكل عام.

and will thereby have abolished its own supremacy as a class.

وبذلك تكون قد ألغت تفوقها كطبقة.

In place of the old Bourgeoisie society, with its classes and class antagonisms, we shall have an association

بدلا من المجتمع البرجوازي القديم، بطبقاته وتناقضاته الطبقية، سيكون لدينا رابطة.

an association in which the free development of each is the condition for the free development of all

جمعية يكون فيها التطور الحر لكل فرد شرطا للتطور الحر للجميع

1) Reactionary Socialism
1) الاشتراكية الرجعية

a) Feudal Socialism
أ) الاشتراكية الإقطاعية

the aristocracies of France and England had a unique historical position

كان للأرستقراطيات في فرنسا وإنجلترا موقع تاريخي فريد

it became their vocation to write pamphlets against modern Bourgeoisie society

أصبحت مهنتهم كتابة كتيبات ضد المجتمع البرجوازي الحديث

In the French revolution of July 1830, and in the English reform agitation

في الثورة الفرنسية في يوليو 1830 ، وفي التحريض على الإصلاح الإنجليزي

these aristocracies again succumbed to the hateful upstart

استسلمت هذه الأرستقراطيات مرة أخرى للمغرور البغيض

Thenceforth, a serious political contest was altogether out of the question

من الآن فصاعدا ، كان التنافس السياسي الجاد غير وارد تماما.

All that remained possible was literary battle, not an actual battle

كل ما تبقى ممكنا هو معركة أدبية وليست معركة فعلية

But even in the domain of literature the old cries of the restoration period had become impossible

ولكن حتى في مجال الأدب ، أصبحت الصرخات القديمة لفترة الاستعادة مستحيلة.

In order to arouse sympathy, the aristocracy were obliged to lose sight, apparently, of their own interests

من أجل إثارة التعاطف ، اضطرت الطبقة الأرستقراطية إلى إغفال مصالحها الخاصة ، على ما يبدو ،

and they were obliged to formulate their indictment against the Bourgeoisie in the interest of the exploited working class

واضطروا إلى صياغة لائحة اتهامهم ضد البرجوازية لصالح الطبقة العاملة المستغلة

Thus the aristocracy took their revenge by singing lampoons on their new master

وهكذا انتقمت الأرستقراطية من خلال غناء السخرية على سيدهم الجديد

and they took their revenge by whispering in his ears sinister prophecies of coming catastrophe

وأخذوا ثأرهم بهمس في أذنيه نبوءات شريرة عن كارثة قادمة

In this way arose Feudal Socialism: half lamentation, half lampoon

بهذه الطريقة نشأت الاشتراكية الإقطاعية: نصف رثاء ، نصف سخرية

it rung as half echo of the past, and projected half menace of the future

لقد رن كنصف صدى للماضي، وتوقع نصف تهديد للمستقبل

at times, by its bitter, witty and incisive criticism, it struck the Bourgeoisie to the very heart's core

في بعض الأحيان ، من خلال نقدها المرير والبارع والقاطع ، ضربت البرجوازية في صميم القلب

but it was always ludicrous in its effect, through total incapacity to comprehend the march of modern history

لكنه كان دائما سخيفا في تأثيره ، من خلال العجز التام عن فهم مسيرة التاريخ الحديث.

The aristocracy, in order to rally the people to them, waved the proletarian alms-bag in front for a banner

الأرستقراطية ، من أجل حشد الناس لهم ، لوحوا بحقيبة الصدقات البروليتارية أمام لافتة

But the people, so often as it joined them, saw on their hindquarters the old feudal coats of arms

لكن الناس ، في كثير من الأحيان عندما انضموا إليهم ، رأوا على مؤخرتهم شعارات النبالة الإقطاعية القديمة.

and they deserted with loud and irreverent laughter

وهجروا بضحك عال وغير موقر

One section of the French Legitimists and "Young England" exhibited this spectacle

عرض قسم واحد من الشرعيين الفرنسيين و "إنجلترا الشابة" هذا المشهد

the feudalists pointed out that their mode of exploitation was different to that of the Bourgeoisie

أشار الإقطاعيون إلى أن طريقة استغلالهم كانت مختلفة عن طريقة
البرجوازية

the feudalists forget that they exploited under circumstances
and conditions that were quite different

ينسى الإقطاعيون أنهم استغلوا في ظل ظروف وظروف مختلفة تماما

and they didn't notice such methods of exploitation are now
antiquated

ولم يلاحظوا أن أساليب الاستغلال هذه أصبحت الآن قديمة

they showed that, under their rule, the modern proletariat
never existed

لقد أظهروا أنه في ظل حكمهم ، لم تكن البروليتاريا الحديثة موجودة أبدا.

but they forget that the modern Bourgeoisie is the necessary
offspring of their own form of society

لكنهم ينسون أن البرجوازية الحديثة هي النسل الضروري لشكلهم الخاص
من المجتمع.

For the rest, they hardly conceal the reactionary character of
their criticism

أما بالنسبة للبقية، فإنهم بالكاد يخفون الطابع الرجعي لانتقاداتهم.

their chief accusation against the Bourgeoisie amounts to the
following

إن اتهامهم الرئيسي ضد البرجوازية يرقى إلى ما يلي:

under the Bourgeoisie regime a social class is being
developed

في ظل النظام البرجوازي يتم تطوير طبقة اجتماعية

this social class is destined to cut up root and branch the old
order of society

هذه الطبقة الاجتماعية مقدر لها أن تقطع جذورها وتتفرع من النظام القديم
للمجتمع

What they upbraid the Bourgeoisie with is not so much that
it creates a proletariat

ما يزعجون به البرجوازية ليس بقدر ما يخلق البروليتاريا.

what they upbraid the Bourgeoisie with is moreso that it
creates a revolutionary proletariat

ما يرفعون به البرجوازية هو أكثر من ذلك أنه يخلق بروليتاريا ثورية

In political practice, therefore, they join in all coercive
measures against the working class

في الممارسة السياسية ، لذلك ، ينضمون إلى جميع التدابير القسرية ضد
الطبقة العاملة

and in ordinary life, despite their highfalutin phrases, they
stoop to pick up the golden apples dropped from the tree of
industry

وفي الحياة العادية ، على الرغم من عباراتهم العالية ، فإنهم ينحدرون
لالتقاط التفاح الذهبي الذي تم إسقاطه من شجرة الصناعة

and they barter truth, love, and honour for commerce in
wool, beetroot-sugar, and potato spirits

وهم يقايضون الحقيقة والحب والشرف بالتجارة في الصوف وسكر
الشمندر وأرواح البطاطس

As the parson has ever gone hand in hand with the landlord,
so has Clerical Socialism with Feudal Socialism

كما سار القسيس جنبا إلى جنب مع المالك ، كذلك فعلت الاشتراكية
الإكليريكية مع الاشتراكية الإقطاعية

Nothing is easier than to give Christian asceticism a Socialist
tinge

ليس هناك ما هو أسهل من إعطاء الزهد المسيحي مسحة اشتراكية

Has not Christianity declaimed against private property,
against marriage, against the State?

ألم تعلن المسيحية ضد الملكية الخاصة ، ضد الزواج ، ضد الدولة؟

Has Christianity not preached in the place of these, charity
and poverty?

ألم تبشر المسيحية بدلا من هذه الصدقة والفقر؟

Does Christianity not preach celibacy and mortification of
the flesh, monastic life and Mother Church?

ألا تبشر المسيحية بالعزوبة وإماتة الجسد والحياة الرهبانية والكنيسة الأم؟

Christian Socialism is but the holy water with which the
priest consecrates the heart-burnings of the aristocrat

الاشتراكية المسيحية ليست سوى الماء المقدس الذي يكرس به الكاهن
حرق قلب الأرستقراطي

b) Petty-Bourgeois Socialism

ب) الاشتراكية البرجوازية الصغيرة

The feudal aristocracy was not the only class that was ruined by the Bourgeoisie

لم تكن الأرستقراطية الإقطاعية هي الطبقة الوحيدة التي دمرتها البرجوازية

it was not the only class whose conditions of existence pined and perished in the atmosphere of modern Bourgeoisie society

لم تكن الطبقة الوحيدة التي كانت ظروف وجودها معلقة وهلكت في جو المجتمع البرجوازي الحديث.

The medieval burgesses and the small peasant proprietors were the precursors of the modern Bourgeoisie

كان البرجيس في العصور الوسطى وصغار الفلاحين المالكين هم سلائف البرجوازية الحديثة

In those countries which are but little developed, industrially and commercially, these two classes still vegetate side by side

في تلك البلدان التي ليست سوى القليل من النمو ، صناعيا وتجاريا ، لا تزال هاتان الفئتان تزرعان جنبا إلى جنب

and in the meantime the Bourgeoisie rise up next to them: industrially, commercially, and politically

وفي هذه الأثناء تنهض البرجوازية بجانبهم: صناعيا وتجاريا وسياسيا.

In countries where modern civilisation has become fully developed, a new class of petty Bourgeoisie has been formed

في البلدان التي أصبحت فيها الحضارة الحديثة متطورة بالكامل ، تم تشكيل طبقة جديدة من البرجوازية الصغيرة

this new social class fluctuates between proletariat and Bourgeoisie

هذه الطبقة الاجتماعية الجديدة تتقلب بين البروليتاريا والبرجوازية

and it is ever renewing itself as a supplementary part of Bourgeoisie society

وهي تجدد نفسها باستمرار كجزء مكمل للمجتمع البرجوازي

The individual members of this class, however, are being constantly hurled down into the proletariat

ومع ذلك ، يتم إلقاء أعضاء هذه الطبقة باستمرار في البروليتاريا

they are sucked up by the proletariat through the action of
competition

يتم امتصاصهم من قبل البروليتاريا من خلال عمل المنافسة

as modern industry develops they even see the moment
approaching when they will completely disappear as an
independent section of modern society

مع تطور الصناعة الحديثة ، يرون حتى اللحظة التي ستختفي فيها تماما
كقسم مستقل من المجتمع الحديث.

they will be replaced, in manufactures, agriculture and
commerce, by overlookers, bailiffs and shopmen

سيتم استبدالهم ، في المصنوعات والزراعة والتجارة ، من قبل المتفرجين
والمحضرين والمتاجرين

In countries like France, where the peasants constitute far
more than half of the population

في بلدان مثل فرنسا ، حيث يشكل الفلاحون أكثر بكثير من نصف السكان

it was natural that there there are writers who sided with the
proletariat against the Bourgeoisie

كان من الطبيعي أن يكون هناك كتاب وقفوا إلى جانب البروليتاريا ضد
البرجوازية

in their criticism of the Bourgeoisie regime they used the
standard of the peasant and petty Bourgeoisie

في نقدهم للنظام البرجوازي استخدموا معيار الفلاحين والبرجوازية
الصغيرة

and from the standpoint of these intermediate classes they
take up the cudgels for the working class

ومن وجهة نظر هذه الطبقات الوسيطة ، فإنهم يأخذون الهراوات للطبقة
العاملة

Thus arose petty-Bourgeoisie Socialism, of which Sismondi
was the head of this school, not only in France but also in
England

وهكذا نشأت الاشتراكية البرجوازية الصغيرة ، التي كان سيسموندي
رئيسا لهذه المدرسة ، ليس فقط في فرنسا ولكن أيضا في إنجلترا.

This school of Socialism dissected with great acuteness the
contradictions in the conditions of modern production

لقد شرحت هذه المدرسة الاشتراكية بحدة شديدة التناقضات في ظروف الإنتاج الحديث.

This school laid bare the hypocritical apologies of economists

كشفت هذه المدرسة عن الاعتذارات المنافقة للاقتصاديين

This school proved, incontrovertibly, the disastrous effects of machinery and division of labour

أثبتت هذه المدرسة ، بشكل لا جدال فيه ، الآثار الكارثية للآلات وتقسيم العمل

it proved the concentration of capital and land in a few hands

أثبتت تركيز رأس المال والأرض في أيدي عدد قليل

it proved how overproduction leads to Bourgeoisie crises

لقد أثبت كيف يؤدي الإفراط في الإنتاج إلى أزمات البرجوازية

it pointed out the inevitable ruin of the petty Bourgeoisie and peasant

وأشار إلى الخراب الحتمي للبرجوازية الصغيرة والفلاحين

the misery of the proletariat, the anarchy in production, the crying inequalities in the distribution of wealth

بؤس البروليتاريا ، والفوضى في الإنتاج ، والتفاوتات المزعجة في توزيع الثروة

it showed how the system of production leads the industrial war of extermination between nations

أظهر كيف يقود نظام الإنتاج حرب الإبادة الصناعية بين الأمم

the dissolution of old moral bonds, of the old family relations, of the old nationalities

انحلال الروابط الأخلاقية القديمة ، والعلاقات الأسرية القديمة ، والقوميات القديمة

In its positive aims, however, this form of Socialism aspires to achieve one of two things

ومع ذلك ، في أهدافه الإيجابية ، يطمح هذا الشكل من الاشتراكية إلى تحقيق أحد أمرين

either it aims to restore the old means of production and of exchange

إما أن يهدف إلى استعادة وسائل الإنتاج والتبادل القديمة.

and with the old means of production it would restore the old property relations, and the old society

ومع وسائل الإنتاج القديمة ، ستعيد علاقات الملكية القديمة والمجتمع القديم

or it aims to cramp the modern means of production and exchange into the old framework of the property relations

أو يهدف إلى تضييق وسائل الإنتاج الحديثة والتبادل في الإطار القديم لعلاقات الملكية

In either case, it is both reactionary and Utopian

في كلتا الحالتين ، فهي رجعية وطوباوية على حد سواء

Its last words are: corporate guilds for manufacture, patriarchal relations in agriculture

كلماتها الأخيرة هي: نقابات الشركات للتصنيع ، والعلاقات الأبوية في الزراعة

Ultimately, when stubborn historical facts had dispersed all intoxicating effects of self-deception

في نهاية المطاف ، عندما بددت الحقائق التاريخية العنيدة كل الآثار المسكرة لخداع الذات

this form of Socialism ended in a miserable fit of pity

انتهى هذا الشكل من الاشتراكية بنوبة بائسة من الشفقة

c) German, or "True," Socialism

ج) الاشتراكية الألمانية أو "الحقيقية"

The Socialist and Communist literature of France originated under the pressure of a Bourgeoisie in power

نشأ الأدب الاشتراكي والشيوعي في فرنسا تحت ضغط البرجوازية في السلطة

and this literature was the expression of the struggle against this power

وكان هذا الأدب تعبيرا عن النضال ضد هذه السلطة

it was introduced into Germany at a time when the Bourgeoisie had just begun its contest with feudal absolutism

تم إدخاله إلى ألمانيا في وقت كانت فيه البرجوازية قد بدأت لتوها صراعها مع الحكم المطلق الإقطاعي

German philosophers, would-be philosophers, and beaux esprits, eagerly seized on this literature

استولى الفلاسفة الألمان ، والفلاسفة المحتملون ، والعفريت الجميلون ، بشغف على هذا الأدب

but they forgot that the writings immigrated from France into Germany without bringing the French social conditions along

لكنهم نسوا أن الكتابات هاجرت من فرنسا إلى ألمانيا دون جلب الظروف الاجتماعية الفرنسية

In contact with German social conditions, this French literature lost all its immediate practical significance

في اتصال مع الظروف الاجتماعية الألمانية ، فقد هذا الأدب الفرنسي كل أهميته العملية المباشرة

and the Communist literature of France assumed a purely literary aspect in German academic circles

واتخذ الأدب الشيوعي الفرنسي جانبا أدبيا بحتا في الأوساط الأكاديمية الألمانية

Thus, the demands of the first French Revolution were nothing more than the demands of "Practical Reason"

وهكذا ، لم تكن مطالب الثورة الفرنسية الأولى أكثر من مطالب "العقل العملي"

and the utterance of the will of the revolutionary French Bourgeoisie signified in their eyes the law of pure Will

ونطق إرادة البرجوازية الفرنسية الثورية يدل في أعينهم على قانون الإرادة الخالصة

it signified Will as it was bound to be; of true human Will generally

كان يدل على الإرادة كما كان لا بد أن يكون. الإرادة البشرية الحقيقية بشكل عام

The world of the German literati consisted solely in bringing the new French ideas into harmony with their ancient philosophical conscience

يتألف عالم الأدباء الألمان فقط من جعل الأفكار الفرنسية الجديدة تنسجم مع ضميرهم الفلسفي القديم.

or rather, they annexed the French ideas without deserting their own philosophic point of view

أو بالأحرى ، ضموا الأفكار الفرنسية دون التخلي عن وجهة نظرهم الفلسفية الخاصة

This annexation took place in the same way in which a foreign language is appropriated, namely, by translation

تم هذا الضم بنفس الطريقة التي يتم بها الاستيلاء على لغة أجنبية ، أي عن طريق الترجمة

It is well known how the monks wrote silly lives of Catholic Saints over manuscripts

من المعروف جيدا كيف كتب الرهبان حياة سخيفة للقديسين الكاثوليك على المخطوطات

the manuscripts on which the classical works of ancient heathendom had been written

المخطوطات التي كتبت عليها الأعمال الكلاسيكية للوثنية القديمة

The German literati reversed this process with the profane French literature

عكس الأدباء الألمان هذه العملية بالأدب الفرنسي المدنس

They wrote their philosophical nonsense beneath the French original

لقد كتبوا هراءهم الفلسفي تحت الأصل الفرنسي

For instance, beneath the French criticism of the economic functions of money, they wrote "Alienation of Humanity"

على سبيل المثال ، تحت النقد الفرنسي للوظائف الاقتصادية للمال ، كتبوا "اغتراب الإنسانية"

beneath the French criticism of the Bourgeoisie State they wrote "dethronement of the Category of the General"

تحت النقد الفرنسي للدولة البرجوازية كتبوا "خلع فئة الجنرال"

The introduction of these philosophical phrases at the back of the French historical criticisms they dubbed:

مقدمة هذه العبارات الفلسفية في الجزء الخلفي من الانتقادات التاريخية الفرنسية التي أطلقوا عليها:

"Philosophy of Action," "True Socialism," "German Science of Socialism," "Philosophical Foundation of Socialism," and so on

"فلسفة العمل" ، "الاشتراكية الحقيقية" ، "علم الاشتراكية الألماني" ، "الأساس الفلسفي للاشتراكية" ، وما إلى ذلك

The French Socialist and Communist literature was thus completely emasculated

وهكذا تم إضعاف الأدب الاشتراكي والشيوعي الفرنسي تماما

in the hands of the German philosophers it ceased to express the struggle of one class with the other

في أيدي الفلاسفة الألمان توقفت عن التعبير عن صراع طبقة واحدة مع الأخرى.

and so the German philosophers felt conscious of having overcome "French one-sidedness"

وهكذا شعر الفلاسفة الألمان بالوعي بأنهم تغلبوا على "الانحياز الفرنسي"

it did not have to represent true requirements, rather, it represented requirements of truth

لم يكن من الضروري أن تمثل المتطلبات الحقيقية ، بل كانت تمثل متطلبات الحقيقة

there was no interest in the proletariat, rather, there was interest in Human Nature

لم يكن هناك اهتمام بالبروليتاريا ، بل كان هناك اهتمام بالطبيعة البشرية

the interest was in Man in general, who belongs to no class, and has no reality

كان الاهتمام بالإنسان بشكل عام ، الذي لا ينتمي إلى طبقة ، وليس له واقع

a man who exists only in the misty realm of philosophical fantasy

رجل موجود فقط في عالم ضبابي من الخيال الفلسفي

but eventually this schoolboy German Socialism also lost its pedantic innocence

ولكن في نهاية المطاف فقدت الاشتراكية الألمانية هذه التلميذة أيضا براءتها المتحذلقة.

the German Bourgeoisie, and especially the Prussian Bourgeoisie fought against feudal aristocracy

حاربت البرجوازية الألمانية ، وخاصة البرجوازية البروسية ضد الأرستقراطية الإقطاعية

the absolute monarchy of Germany and Prussia was also being faught against

كما تم محاربة الملكية المطلقة لألمانيا وبروسيا

and in turn, the literature of the liberal movement also became more earnest

وفي المقابل ، أصبحت أدبيات الحركة الليبرالية أكثر جدية

Germany's long wished-for opportunity for "true" Socialism was offered

تم تقديم فرصة ألمانيا التي طال انتظارها للاشتراكية "الحقيقية"

the opportunity of confronting the political movement with the Socialist demands

فرصة مواجهة الحركة السياسية بالمطالب الاشتراكية

the opportunity of hurling the traditional anathemas against liberalism

فرصة إلقاء اللعنة التقليدية ضد الليبرالية

the opportunity to attack representative government and Bourgeoisie competition

فرصة لمهاجمة الحكومة التمثيلية والمنافسة البرجوازية

Bourgeoisie freedom of the press, Bourgeoisie legislation, Bourgeoisie liberty and equality

حرية الصحافة البرجوازية، التشريعات البرجوازية، الحرية والمساواة البرجوازية

all of these could now be critiqued in the real world, rather than in fantasy

كل هذه الأمور يمكن الآن نقدها في العالم الحقيقي ، وليس في الخيال

feudal aristocracy and absolute monarchy had long preached to the masses

لطالما بشرت الأرستقراطية الإقطاعية والملكية المطلقة للجماهير

"the working man has nothing to lose, and he has everything to gain"

"الرجل العامل ليس لديه ما يخسره ، ولديه كل شيء يكسبه"

the Bourgeoisie movement also offered a chance to confront these platitudes

كما قدمت الحركة البرجوازية فرصة لمواجهة هذه التفاهات.

the French criticism presupposed the existence of modern Bourgeoisie society

افترض النقد الفرنسي وجود مجتمع برجوازي حديث

Bourgeoisie economic conditions of existence and Bourgeoisie political constitution

شروط الوجود الاقتصادية البرجوازية والدستور السياسي البرجوازي

the very things whose attainment was the object of the pending struggle in Germany

الأشياء ذاتها التي كان تحقيقها موضوع النضال المعلق في ألمانيا

Germany's silly echo of socialism abandoned these goals just in the nick of time

لقد تخلى صدى ألمانيا السخيف للاشتراكية عن هذه الأهداف في الوقت المناسب

the absolute governments had their following of parsons, professors, country squires and officials

كان للحكومات المطلقة أتباعها من بارسونز والأساتذة و Squires البلد والمسؤولين

the government of the time met the German working-class risings with floggings and bullets

قابلت الحكومة في ذلك الوقت انتفاضات الطبقة العاملة الألمانية بالجلد والرصاص

for them this socialism served as a welcome scarecrow against the threatening Bourgeoisie

بالنسبة لهم كانت هذه الاشتراكية بمثابة فزاعة مرحب بها ضد البرجوازية المهددة.

and the German government was able to offer a sweet dessert after the bitter pills it handed out

وتمكنت الحكومة الألمانية من تقديم حلوى حلوة بعد الحبوب المرة التي
وزعتها

this "True" Socialism thus served the governments as a
weapon for fighting the German Bourgeoisie

وهكذا خدمت هذه الاشتراكية "الحقيقية" الحكومات كسلاح لمحاربة
البرجوازية الألمانية

and, at the same time, it directly represented a reactionary
interest; that of the German Philistines

وفي الوقت نفسه ، مثلت بشكل مباشر مصلحة رجعية. أن من الفلسطينيين
الألمان

In Germany the petty Bourgeoisie class is the real social
basis of the existing state of things

في ألمانيا الطبقة البرجوازية الصغيرة هي الأساس الاجتماعي الحقيقي
للحالة القائمة للأشياء.

a relique of the sixteenth century that has constantly been
cropping up under various forms

من بقايا القرن السادس عشر التي كانت تظهر باستمرار تحت أشكال
مختلفة

To preserve this class is to preserve the existing state of
things in Germany

الحفاظ على هذه الطبقة هو الحفاظ على الحالة الحالية للأشياء في ألمانيا

The industrial and political supremacy of the Bourgeoisie
threatens the petty Bourgeoisie with certain destruction

إن التفوق الصناعي والسياسي للبرجوازية يهدد البرجوازية الصغيرة
بتدمير معين

on the one hand, it threatens to destroy the petty Bourgeoisie
through the concentration of capital

فمن ناحية، يهدد بتدمير البرجوازية الصغيرة من خلال تركيز رأس المال.

on the other hand, the Bourgeoisie threatens to destroy it
through the rise of a revolutionary proletariat

من ناحية أخرى ، تهدد البرجوازية بتدميرها من خلال صعود البروليتاريا
الثورية

"True" Socialism appeared to kill these two birds with one
stone. It spread like an epidemic

يبدو أن الاشتراكية "الحقيقية" تقتل هذين العصفورين بحجر واحد. انتشر
مثل الوباء

The robe of speculative cobwebs, embroidered with flowers of rhetoric, steeped in the dew of sickly sentiment

رداء خيوط العنكبوت المضاربة ، مطرزة بزهور الخطابة ، غارقة في ندى المشاعر المريضة

this transcendental robe in which the German Socialists wrapped their sorry "eternal truths"

هذا الرداء المتسامي الذي لف فيه الاشتراكيون الألمان "حقائقهم الأبدية" المؤسفة

all skin and bone, served to wonderfully increase the sale of their goods amongst such a public

كل الجلد والعظام ، عملت على زيادة بيع سلعهم بشكل رائع بين مثل هذا الجمهور

And on its part, German Socialism recognised, more and more, its own calling

ومن جانبها ، اعترفت الاشتراكية الألمانية ، أكثر فأكثر ، بدعوتها الخاصة.

it was called to be the bombastic representative of the petty-Bourgeoisie Philistine

تم استدعاؤه ليكون الممثل المنمق للبرجوازية الصغيرة الفلسطينية

It proclaimed the German nation to be the model nation, and German petty Philistine the model man

أعلنت أن الأمة الألمانية هي الأمة النموذجية ، والفلسطيني الألماني الصغير هو الرجل النموذجي

To every villainous meanness of this model man it gave a hidden, higher, Socialistic interpretation

لكل خسة خسيسة لهذا الرجل النموذجي أعطت تفسيرا اشتراكيا خفيا وأعلى

this higher, Socialistic interpretation was the exact contrary of its real character

كان هذا التفسير الاشتراكي الأعلى هو النقيض التام لطابعه الحقيقي

It went to the extreme length of directly opposing the "brutally destructive" tendency of Communism

لقد ذهب إلى أقصى حد من المعارضة المباشرة للنزعة الشيوعية "المدمرة بوحشية"

and it proclaimed its supreme and impartial contempt of all class struggles

وأعلنت ازدراءها الأسمى والمحايد لجميع الصراعات الطبقية

With very few exceptions, all the so-called Socialist and
Communist publications that now (1847) circulate in
Germany belong to the domain of this foul and enervating
literature

مع استثناءات قليلة جدا ، فإن جميع المنشورات الاشتراكية والشيوعية
المزعومة التي يتم تداولها الآن (1847) في ألمانيا تنتمي إلى مجال هذا
الأدب البغيض والمزعج.

2) Conservative Socialism, or Bourgeoisie Socialism
الاشتراكية المحافظة ، أو الاشتراكية البرجوازية

A part of the Bourgeoisie is desirous of redressing social grievances

جزء من البرجوازية يرغب في معالجة المظالم الاجتماعية

in order to secure the continued existence of Bourgeoisie society

من أجل ضمان استمرار وجود المجتمع البرجوازي

To this section belong economists, philanthropists, humanitarians

ينتمي إلى هذا القسم الاقتصاديون والمحسنون والعاملون في المجال الإنساني

improvers of the condition of the working class and organisers of charity

محسنو أوضاع الطبقة العاملة ومنظمو الأعمال الخيرية

members of societies for the prevention of cruelty to animals

أعضاء جمعيات منع القسوة على

temperance fanatics, hole-and-corner reformers of every imaginable kind

المتعصبون للاعتدال ، مصلحو الثقب والزاوية من كل نوع يمكن تخيله

This form of Socialism has, moreover, been worked out into complete systems

علاوة على ذلك ، تم تطوير هذا الشكل من الاشتراكية في أنظمة كاملة

We may cite Proudhon's "Philosophie de la Misère" as an example of this form

يمكننا الاستشهاد ب "فلسفة البؤس" لبرودون كمثال على هذا الشكل

The Socialistic Bourgeoisie want all the advantages of modern social conditions

البرجوازية الاشتراكية تريد كل مزايا الظروف الاجتماعية الحديثة

but the Socialistic Bourgeoisie don't necessarily want the resulting struggles and dangers

لكن البرجوازية الاشتراكية لا تريد بالضرورة بالنضالات والمخاطر الناتجة

They desire the existing state of society, minus its revolutionary and disintegrating elements

إنهم يرغبون في الحالة القائمة للمجتمع ، باستثناء عناصره الثورية والمتفككة

in other words, they wish for a Bourgeoisie without a proletariat

وبعبارة أخرى، فإنهم يرغبون في برجوازية بدون بروليتاريا.

The Bourgeoisie naturally conceives the world in which it is supreme to be the best

تتصور البرجوازية بشكل طبيعي العالم الذي يكون فيه الأفضل

and Bourgeoisie Socialism develops this comfortable conception into various more or less complete systems

والاشتراكية البرجوازية تطور هذا المفهوم المريح إلى أنظمة مختلفة أكثر أو أقل اكتمالا

they would very much like the proletariat to march straightway into the social New Jerusalem

إنهم يرغبون بشدة في أن تسير البروليتاريا مباشرة إلى القدس الجديدة الاجتماعية

but in reality it requires the proletariat to remain within the bounds of existing society

لكنه في الواقع يتطلب من البروليتاريا أن تبقى داخل حدود المجتمع القائم.

they ask the proletariat to cast away all their hateful ideas concerning the Bourgeoisie

يطلبون من البروليتاريا التخلص من كل أفكارهم البغيضة المتعلقة بالبرجوازية

there is a second more practical, but less systematic, form of this Socialism

هناك شكل ثان أكثر عملية ، ولكنه أقل منهجية ، لهذه الاشتراكية

this form of socialism sought to depreciate every revolutionary movement in the eyes of the working class

سعى هذا الشكل من الاشتراكية إلى التقليل من قيمة كل حركة ثورية في نظر الطبقة العاملة.

they argue no mere political reform could be of any advantage to them

وهم يجادلون بأن مجرد الإصلاح السياسي لا يمكن أن يكون مفيدا لهم.

only a change in the material conditions of existence in economic relations are of benefit

فقط تغيير في الظروف المادية للوجود في العلاقات الاقتصادية هي ذات فائدة

like communism, this form of socialism advocates for a change in the material conditions of existence

مثل الشيوعية ، يدعو هذا الشكل من الاشتراكية إلى تغيير الظروف المادية للوجود

however, this form of socialism by no means suggests the abolition of the Bourgeoisie relations of production

ومع ذلك ، فإن هذا الشكل من الاشتراكية لا يوحي بأي حال من الأحوال بإلغاء علاقات الإنتاج البرجوازية.

the abolition of the Bourgeoisie relations of production can only be achieved through a revolution

لا يمكن إلغاء علاقات الإنتاج البرجوازية إلا من خلال الثورة

but instead of a revolution, this form of socialism suggests administrative reforms

ولكن بدلا من الثورة ، يقترح هذا الشكل من الاشتراكية إصلاحات إدارية

and these administrative reforms would be based on the continued existence of these relations

وستستند هذه الإصلاحات الإدارية إلى استمرار وجود هذه العلاقات

reforms, therefore, that in no respect affect the relations between capital and labour

الإصلاحات ، لذلك ، لا تؤثر بأي شكل من الأشكال على العلاقات بين رأس المال والعمل

at best, such reforms lessen the cost and simplify the administrative work of Bourgeoisie government

في أحسن الأحوال، تقلل هذه الإصلاحات من التكلفة وتبسط العمل الإداري للحكومة البرجوازية.

Bourgeois Socialism attains adequate expression, when, and only when, it becomes a mere figure of speech

الاشتراكية البرجوازية تصل إلى التعبير المناسب ، عندما ، وفقط عندما تصبح مجرد شكل من أشكال الكلام

Free trade: for the benefit of the working class

التجارة الحرة: لصالح الطبقة العاملة

Protective duties: for the benefit of the working class

واجبات الحماية: لصالح الطبقة العاملة

Prison Reform: for the benefit of the working class

إصلاح السجون: لصالح الطبقة العاملة

This is the last word and the only seriously meant word of Bourgeoisie Socialism

هذه هي الكلمة الأخيرة والكلمة الوحيدة الجادة للاشتراكية البرجوازية.

It is summed up in the phrase: the Bourgeoisie is a Bourgeoisie for the benefit of the working class

تتلخص في العبارة: البرجوازية هي برجوازية لصالح الطبقة العاملة

3) Critical-Utopian Socialism and Communism
الاشتراكية الطوباوية النقدية والشيوعية

We do not here refer to that literature which has always given voice to the demands of the proletariat

نحن لا نشير هنا إلى ذلك الأدب الذي أعطى دائما صوتا لمطالب البروليتاريا.

this has been present in every great modern revolution, such as the writings of Babeuf and others

وقد كان هذا حاضرا في كل ثورة حديثة عظيمة مثل كتابات بابوف وغيرها.

The first direct attempts of the proletariat to attain its own ends necessarily failed

المحاولات المباشرة الأولى للبروليتاريا لتحقيق غاياتها الخاصة فشلت بالضرورة

these attempts were made in times of universal excitement, when feudal society was being overthrown

جرت هذه المحاولات في أوقات الإثارة العالمية ، عندما تم الإطاحة بالمجتمع الإقطاعي

the then undeveloped state of the proletariat led to those attempts failing

أدت حالة البروليتاريا غير المتطورة آنذاك إلى فشل تلك المحاولات

and they failed due to the absence of the economic conditions for its emancipation

وفشلوا بسبب غياب الظروف الاقتصادية لتحررها

conditions that had yet to be produced, and could be produced by the impending Bourgeoisie epoch alone

الظروف التي لم يتم إنتاجها بعد ، ويمكن أن تنتجها الحقبة البرجوازية الوشيكة وحدها

The revolutionary literature that accompanied these first movements of the proletariat had necessarily a reactionary character

كان للأدب الثوري الذي رافق هذه الحركات الأولى للبروليتاريا بالضرورة طابع رجعي

This literature inculcated universal asceticism and social levelling in its crudest form

غرس هذا الأدب الزهد العالمي والتسوية الاجتماعية في أكثر أشكالها فظاظة

The Socialist and Communist systems, properly so called, spring into existence in the early undeveloped period

إن النظامين الاشتراكي والشيوعي ، ما يسمى بشكل صحيح ، ينبثقان إلى الوجود في أوائل الفترة غير المتطورة.

Saint-Simon, Fourier, Owen and others, described the struggle between proletariat and Bourgeoisie (see Section 1)

وصف سان سيمون وفورييه وأوين وآخرون الصراع بين البروليتاريا والبرجوازية (انظر القسم 1)

The founders of these systems see, indeed, the class antagonisms

يرى مؤسسو هذه الأنظمة ، في الواقع ، العداوات الطبقية

they also see the action of the decomposing elements, in the prevailing form of society

كما يرون عمل العناصر المتحللة ، في الشكل السائد للمجتمع

But the proletariat, as yet in its infancy, offers to them the spectacle of a class without any historical initiative

لكن البروليتاريا ، التي لا تزال في مهدها ، تقدم لهم مشهد طبقة دون أي مبادرة تاريخية

they see the spectacle of a social class without any independent political movement

يرون مشهد طبقة اجتماعية بدون أي حركة سياسية مستقلة

the development of class antagonism keeps even pace with the development of industry

تطور العداء الطبقي يواكب تطور الصناعة

so the economic situation does not as yet offer to them the material conditions for the emancipation of the proletariat

لذا فإن الوضع الاقتصادي لا يوفر لهم بعد الظروف المادية لتحرير البروليتاريا.

They therefore search after a new social science, after new social laws, that are to create these conditions

لذلك يبحثون عن علم اجتماعي جديد ، بعد قوانين اجتماعية جديدة ، من شأنها أن تخلق هذه الظروف.

historical action is to yield to their personal inventive action

العمل التاريخي هو الخضوع لعملهم الإبداعي الشخصي

historically created conditions of emancipation are to yield to fantastic conditions

شروط التحرر التي تم إنشاؤها تاريخيا هي الخضوع لظروف رائعة

and the gradual, spontaneous class-organisation of the proletariat is to yield to the organisation of society

والتنظيم الطبقي التدريجي والعفوي للبروليتاريا هو الخضوع لتنظيم المجتمع

the organisation of society specially contrived by these inventors

تنظيم المجتمع الذي ابتكره هؤلاء المخترعون خصيصا

Future history resolves itself, in their eyes, into the propaganda and the practical carrying out of their social plans

التاريخ المستقبلي يحل نفسه ، في نظرهم ، في الدعاية والتنفيذ العملي لخططهم الاجتماعية

In the formation of their plans they are conscious of caring chiefly for the interests of the working class

في صياغة خططهم ، يدركون الاهتمام بشكل رئيسي بمصالح الطبقة العاملة

Only from the point of view of being the most suffering class does the proletariat exist for them

فقط من وجهة نظر كونهم الطبقة الأكثر معاناة توجد البروليتاريا بالنسبة لهم

The undeveloped state of the class struggle and their own surroundings inform their opinions

إن الحالة غير المتطورة للصراع الطبقي ومحيطهم الخاص يعلمون آراءهم

Socialists of this kind consider themselves far superior to all class antagonisms

يعتبر الاشتراكيون من هذا النوع أنفسهم أفضل بكثير من جميع العداوات الطبقية.

They want to improve the condition of every member of society, even that of the most favoured

إنهم يريدون تحسين حالة كل فرد من أفراد المجتمع ، حتى أولئك الأكثر حظا

Hence, they habitually appeal to society at large, without distinction of class

ومن ثم ، فإنهم عادة ما يناشدون المجتمع ككل ، دون تمييز طبقي

nay, they appeal to society at large by preference to the ruling class

كلا ، إنهم يناشدون المجتمع ككل من خلال تفضيل الطبقة الحاكمة

to them, all it requires is for others to understand their system

بالنسبة لهم ، كل ما يتطلبه الأمر هو أن يفهم الآخرون نظامهم

because how can people fail to see that the best possible plan is for the best possible state of society?

لأنه كيف يمكن للناس أن يفشلوا في رؤية أن أفضل خطة ممكنة هي لأفضل حالة ممكنة للمجتمع؟

Hence, they reject all political, and especially all revolutionary, action

ومن ثم فهم يرفضون كل عمل سياسي، وخاصة كل عمل ثوري.

they wish to attain their ends by peaceful means

إنهم يرغبون في تحقيق غاياتهم بالوسائل السلمية

they endeavour, by small experiments, which are necessarily doomed to failure

إنهم يسعون ، من خلال تجارب صغيرة ، محكوم عليها بالضرورة بالفشل

and by the force of example they try to pave the way for the new social Gospel

وبقوة المثال يحاولون تمهيد الطريق للإنجيل الاجتماعي الجديد

Such fantastic pictures of future society, painted at a time when the proletariat is still in a very undeveloped state

هذه الصور الرائعة للمجتمع المستقبلي ، رسمت في وقت لا تزال فيه البروليتاريا في حالة غير متطورة للغاية

and it still has but a fantastical conception of its own position

ولا يزال لديها تصور خيالي لموقفها الخاص

but their first instinctive yearnings correspond with the yearnings of the proletariat

لكن أشواقهم الغريزية الأولى تتوافق مع تطلعات البروليتاريا

both yearn for a general reconstruction of society

كلاهما يتوق إلى إعادة بناء عامة للمجتمع

But these Socialist and Communist publications also contain a critical element

لكن هذه المنشورات الاشتراكية والشيوعية تحتوي أيضا على عنصر جاسم

They attack every principle of existing society

إنهم يهاجمون كل مبدأ من مبادئ المجتمع القائم

Hence they are full of the most valuable materials for the enlightenment of the working class

ومن ثم فهي مليئة بالمواد الأكثر قيمة لتنوير الطبقة العاملة

they propose abolition of the distinction between town and country, and the family

يقترحون إلغاء التمييز بين المدينة والريف والأسرة

the abolition of the carrying on of industries for the account of private individuals

إلغاء مزاولة الصناعات لحساب الأفراد

and the abolition of the wage system and the proclamation of social harmony

وإلغاء نظام الأجور وإعلان الوئام الاجتماعي

the conversion of the functions of the State into a mere superintendence of production

تحويل وظائف الدولة إلى مجرد إشراف على الإنتاج

all these proposals, point solely to the disappearance of class antagonisms

كل هذه المقترحات تشير فقط إلى اختفاء العداوات الطبقية.

class antagonisms were, at that time, only just cropping up

كانت الخصومات الطبقية ، في ذلك الوقت ، مجرد ظهور

in these publications these class antagonisms are recognised in their earliest, indistinct and undefined forms only

في هذه المنشورات ، يتم التعرف على هذه التناقضات الطبقية في أشكالها المبكرة وغير الواضحة وغير المحددة فقط

These proposals, therefore, are of a purely Utopian character

وبالتالي ، فإن هذه المقترحات ذات طابع طوباوي بحت.

The significance of Critical-Utopian Socialism and Communism bears an inverse relation to historical development

تحمل أهمية الاشتراكية الطوباوية النقدية والشيوعية علاقة عكسية بالتطور التاريخي

the modern class struggle will develop and continue to take
definite shape

سوف يتطور الصراع الطبقي الحديث ويستمر في اتخاذ شكل محدد

this fantastic standing from the contest will lose all practical
value

هذا الموقف الرائع من المسابقة سيفقد كل قيمة عملية

these fantastic attacks on class antagonisms will lose all
theoretical justification

هذه الهجمات الخيالية على العداوات الطبقية ستفقد كل مبرر نظري

the originators of these systems were, in many respects,
revolutionary

كان منشئو هذه الأنظمة ، في كثير من النواحي ، ثوريين

but their disciples have, in every case, formed mere
reactionary sects

لكن تلاميذهم شكلوا في كل حالة مجرد طوائف رجعية.

They hold tightly to the original views of their masters

إنهم يتمسكون بشدة بالآراء الأصلية لأسيادهم

but these views are in opposition to the progressive
historical development of the proletariat

لكن هذه الآراء تتعارض مع التطور التاريخي التدريجي للبروليتاريا.

They, therefore, endeavour, and that consistently, to deaden
the class struggle

لذلك ، يسعون ، وذلك باستمرار ، إلى إخماد الصراع الطبقي

and they consistently endeavour to reconcile the class
antagonisms

وهم يسعون باستمرار إلى التوفيق بين التناقضات الطبقية.

They still dream of experimental realisation of their social
Utopias

ما زالوا يحلمون بالتحقيق التجريبي لليوتوبيا الاجتماعية الخاصة بهم

they still dream of founding isolated "phalansteres" and
establishing "Home Colonies"

ما زالوا يحلمون بتأسيس "كتائب" معزولة وإنشاء "مستعمرات منزلية"

they dream of setting up a "Little Icaria"—duodecimo
editions of the New Jerusalem

يحلمون بإنشاء "إيكاريا الصغيرة" - طبعات ثنائية من القدس الجديدة

and they dream to realise all these castles in the air

ويحلمون بتحقيق كل هذه القلاع في الهواء

they are compelled to appeal to the feelings and purses of
the bourgeois

إنهم مجبرون على مناشدة مشاعر ومحافظ البرجوازية

By degrees they sink into the category of the reactionary
conservative Socialists depicted above

بالدرجات يغرقون في فئة الاشتراكيين المحافظين الرجعيين الموضحين
أعلاه

they differ from these only by more systematic pedantry

أنها تختلف عن هذه فقط من خلال التحذلق أكثر منهجية

and they differ by their fanatical and superstitious belief in
the miraculous effects of their social science

ويختلفون بإيمانهم المتعصب والخرافي بالآثار المعجزة لعلمهم الاجتماعي.

They, therefore, violently oppose all political action on the
part of the working class

لذلك ، يعارضون بعنف جميع الإجراءات السياسية من جانب الطبقة
العاملة

such action, according to them, can only result from blind
unbelief in the new Gospel

مثل هذا العمل ، وفقا لهم ، لا يمكن أن ينتج إلا عن عدم الإيمان الأعمى
بالإنجيل الجديد

The Owenites in England, and the Fourierists in France,
respectively, oppose the Chartists and the "Réformistes"

يعارض الأوينيون في إنجلترا ، والفورييه في فرنسا ، على التوالي ،
الشارتيين و "الإصلاحيين"

Position of the Communists in Relation to the Various Existing Opposision Parties

موقف الشيوعيين من مختلف الأحزاب المعارضة القائمة

Section II has made clear the relations of the Communists to the existing working-class parties

وقد أوضح القسم الثاني علاقات الشيوعيين بأحزاب الطبقة العاملة القائمة.

such as the Chartists in England, and the Agrarian Reformers in America

مثل Chartists في إنجلترا ، والإصلاحيين الزراعيين في أمريكا

The Communists fight for the attainment of the immediate aims

الشيوعيون يناضلون من أجل تحقيق الأهداف المباشرة

they fight for the enforcement of the momentary interests of the working class

إنهم يناضلون من أجل فرض المصالح اللحظية للطبقة العاملة

but in the political movement of the present, they also represent and take care of the future of that movement

لكن في الحركة السياسية في الوقت الحاضر ، يمثلون أيضا مستقبل تلك الحركة ويهتمون به

In France the Communists ally themselves with the Social-Democrats

في فرنسا يتحالف الشيوعيون مع الاشتراكيين الديمقراطيين

and they position themselves against the conservative and radical Bourgeoisie

ويضعون أنفسهم ضد البرجوازية المحافظة والراديكالية

however, they reserve the right to take up a critical position in regard to phrases and illusions traditionally handed down from the great Revolution

ومع ذلك ، فإنهم يحتفظون بالحق في اتخاذ موقف نقدي فيما يتعلق بالعبارات والأوهام التي تم تسليمها تقليديا من الثورة العظيمة

In Switzerland they support the Radicals, without losing sight of the fact that this party consists of antagonistic elements

في سويسرا يدعمون الراديكاليين ، دون إغفال حقيقة أن هذا الحزب يتكون من عناصر معادية.

partly of Democratic Socialists, in the French sense, partly of radical Bourgeoisie

جزء من الاشتراكيين الديمقراطيين ، بالمعنى الفرنسي ، جزئيا من البرجوازية الراديكالية

In Poland they support the party that insists on an agrarian revolution as the prime condition for national emancipation

في بولندا يدعمون الحزب الذي يصر على الثورة الزراعية كشرط رئيسي للتحرر الوطني.

that party which fomented the insurrection of Cracow in 1846

ذلك الحزب الذي حرض على تمرد كراكوف في عام 1846

In Germany they fight with the Bourgeoisie whenever it acts in a revolutionary way

في ألمانيا يناضلون مع البرجوازية كلما تصرفت بطريقة ثورية.

against the absolute monarchy, the feudal squirearchy, and the petty Bourgeoisie

ضد الملكية المطلقة ، والإقطاعية الإقطاعية ، والبرجوازية الصغيرة

But they never cease, for a single instant, to instil into the working class one particular idea

لكنهم لا يتوقفون أبدا ، للحظة واحدة ، عن غرس فكرة معينة في الطبقة العاملة.

the clearest possible recognition of the hostile antagonism between Bourgeoisie and proletariat

أوضح اعتراف ممكن بالعداء العدائي بين البرجوازية والبروليتاريا

so that the German workers may straightaway use the weapons at their disposal

حتى يتمكن العمال الألمان على الفور من استخدام الأسلحة الموجودة تحت تصرفهم

the social and political conditions that the Bourgeoisie must necessarily introduce along with its supremacy

الظروف الاجتماعية والسياسية التي يجب على البرجوازية إدخالها بالضرورة جنبا إلى جنب مع تفوقها

the fall of the reactionary classes in Germany is inevitable

سقوط الطبقات الرجعية في ألمانيا أمر لا مفر منه

and then the fight against the Bourgeoisie itself may immediately begin

ومن ثم قد تبدأ المعركة ضد البرجوازية نفسها على الفور

The Communists turn their attention chiefly to Germany, because that country is on the eve of a Bourgeoisie revolution

يوجه الشيوعيون انتباههم بشكل رئيسي إلى ألمانيا ، لأن هذا البلد على أعتاب ثورة برجوازية.

a revolution that is bound to be carried out under more advanced conditions of European civilisation

ثورة لا بد أن تتم في ظل ظروف أكثر تقدما للحضارة الأوروبية

and it is bound to be carried out with a much more developed proletariat

ومن المحتم أن يتم تنفيذه مع بروليتاريا أكثر تطورا

a proletariat more advanced than that of England was in the seventeenth, and of France in the eighteenth century

كانت البروليتاريا أكثر تقدما من تلك التي كانت في إنجلترا في القرن السابع عشر ، وفرنسا في القرن الثامن عشر

and because the Bourgeoisie revolution in Germany will be but the prelude to an immediately following proletarian revolution

ولأن الثورة البرجوازية في ألمانيا لن تكون سوى مقدمة لثورة بروليتارية تالية مباشرة

In short, the Communists everywhere support every revolutionary movement against the existing social and political order of things

باختصار، يدعم الشيوعيون في كل مكان كل حركة ثورية ضد النظام الاجتماعي والسياسي القائم.

In all these movements they bring to the front, as the leading question in each, the property question

في كل هذه الحركات يجلبونها إلى الواجهة ، كسؤال رئيسي في كل منها ، مسألة الملكية

no matter what its degree of development is in that country at the time

بغض النظر عن درجة تطورها في ذلك البلد في ذلك الوقت

Finally, they labour everywhere for the union and agreement of the democratic parties of all countries

وأخيرا، فإنهم يعملون في كل مكان من أجل اتحاد واتفاق الأحزاب الديمقراطية في جميع البلدان.

The Communists disdain to conceal their views and aims

الشيوعيون يزدرون إخفاء آرائهم وأهدافهم

They openly declare that their ends can be attained only by the forcible overthrow of all existing social conditions

إنهم يعلنون صراحة أنه لا يمكن تحقيق غاياتهم إلا من خلال الإطاحة القسرية بجميع الظروف الاجتماعية القائمة.

Let the ruling classes tremble at a Communistic revolution

دع الطبقات الحاكمة ترتجف من الثورة الشيوعية

The proletarians have nothing to lose but their chains

ليس لدى البروليتاريين ما يخسرونه سوى قيودهم

They have a world to win

لديهم عالم للفوز به

WORKING MEN OF ALL COUNTRIES, UNITE!

أيها العمال من جميع البلدان، اتحدوا!